Advance Praise for
An Entrepreneur's Manifesto

"*An Entrepreneur's Manifesto* beautifully illustrates the mandate to nourish and develop an entrepreneurial mindset for a new entrepreneurial generation, empowering individuals by tapping into their passion."
—Diana Davis Spencer, chairman and president of the
Diana Davis Spencer Foundation

"In the next few decades, billions of young people will enter the global workforce. There are not jobs waiting for most of them, especially those who are low-income. I believe that entrepreneurship education is the best solution, and this book explains why!"
—Michael Simmons, cofounder of Empact, *Forbes* columnist,
and author of *The Student Success Manifesto: How to Create
a Life of Passion, Purpose, and Prosperity*

"One walks away from this book with a sense of urgency to ensure that entrepreneurial education becomes a mainstay in the halls of all schools and places of education."
—Rabbi Yehoshua Werde, director of
Crown Heights Young Entrepreneurs

"Through story, experience, and data, Mariotti makes it clear that entrepreneurship is the way to both reinvigorate our economy and redirect men and women away from legacies of incarceration and desperation and towards a promising, self-created career."
—Catherine Hoke, founder and CEO of Defy Ventures

"With *An Entrepreneur's Manifesto*, Steve Mariotti further enhances his reputation as a change agent. This powerful book can transform thinking, lives, and entire communities."
—Sheila Rule, cofounder of the Think Outside the Cell Foundation; former senior editor, *The New York Times*

"Entrepreneurship is the only real way for people to get out of poverty. The prestige of a successful business builds incredible self-respect that also has many benefits to society as a whole. Even business initiatives that are not successful still bring solid life experiences and serve as a base for subsequent efforts. Steve Mariotti's latest book brings it all together. I highly recommend everyone read the book and join the 'revolution.'"
—Gary Voight, CEO of CorasWorks

"The light of entrepreneurship is a guide to freedom and hope for young people from all corners of the earth, from all walks of life. *An Entrepreneur's Manifesto* is the twenty-first century economic blueprint we've been waiting for."
—Joseph Robinson, author of *Think Outside the Cell: An Entrepreneur's Guide for the Incarcerated and Formerly Incarcerated*

"*An Entrepreneur's Manifesto* is destined to be a classic for my generation. Steve Mariotti has not only had a huge impact in causing entrepreneurship education to be taken seriously but he has inspired countless individuals, including myself, toward making an impact in that field. The significance of the insights he shares in this book cannot be overstated."
—Sheena Lindhal, CEO and cofounder of Empact

AN ENTREPRENEUR'S MANIFESTO

WITHDRAWN

AN ENTREPRENEUR'S
MANIFESTO

Steve Mariotti

TEMPLETON PRESS

This book is dedicated to every NFTE student, teacher, supporter, donor, and board member. Thank you for having given my life meaning and purpose for a wonderful twenty-seven years.

Contents

Preface

Entrepreneurship education can be a societal change agent,
a great enabler in all sectors. Not everyone needs to become an
entrepreneur to benefit from more entrepreneurial education,
but all members of society need to be more entrepreneurial.

—MUHAMMAD YUNUS, 2006 NOBEL PEACE PRIZE WINNER

THE PURPOSE of this book is to start a revolution. An Entrepreneurship Revolution. The goal: To create a global "entrepreneurial ecosystem" that will provide every young person in the world with the knowledge, skills, and tools to create and operate a small business.

A child drops out of high school in the United States every nine seconds. . . . Imagine the positive impact on our economy if he or she didn't. Imagine if every child, worldwide, were business literate enough to find his or her own pathway to prosperity. Unlocking the entrepreneurial creativity of at-risk youth could change the world.

I believe this pathway to prosperity can end poverty as we currently know it within two generations. This may sound utopian, but it's not. It is based on a hardheaded calculation: If we can cut the rate of new business failure by even 1 to 2 percent, we put ourselves on a glide path to eliminate poverty within the next two generations.

Entrepreneurship education is also the most practical way to address so many of the ills plaguing the world economy today, from underemployment to the wealth gap.

If the Entrepreneurship Revolution has a manifesto, it is this: The most political act a person can ever do is to create a business. To acquire an asset or skill and then sell the product or service to another human being is a revolutionary act, an act that has the power to transform lives, rebuild families, and forever change communities.

This revolution does not seek to change the essence of human nature like the blood-soaked ideologues of the twentieth century attempted to do. This revolution will not try remake the human spirit in the vision of a favored few. My intellectual heroes—Milton Friedman, Friedrich Hayek and Ludwig von Mises—explicitly rejected the bullying, antihumanist thinking promoted by Karl Marx, Vladimir Lenin, and Frantz Fanon in favor of intellectual and economic freedom for all.

The Entrepreneurship Revolution is a revolution of consciousness; it is an awakening of the natural inventiveness, creativity, and desire for freedom deeply rooted in the psyche of every human being.

This is a capitalist revolution, but one enhanced and energized by new understandings of the nature of twenty-first-century entrepreneurship and how to transmit this knowledge to rising generations of business creators around the globe. In this book, I'll survey exciting new efforts to encourage entrepreneurship globally, including in some of the world's poorest communities. There has been an explosion in the academic field of entrepreneurial research in the last three decades. We'll explore the latest data on attitudes toward business formation and risk taking and how these affect economies. And I'll look closely at how and why entrepreneurship transforms countries, communities, and people.

I have seen such transformations countless times in my nearly three decades of work with the Network for Teaching Entrepreneurship (NFTE), the nonprofit I founded in 1982 to bring entrepreneurship education to at-risk youth. Back then I was a desperate (and failing) special-education teacher in the New York City public school system. I was unable to reach or teach the out-of-control students in my Bed-Stuy high school. On the verge of giving up, I stepped out of the classroom in frustration one day and, in a final desperate move, took off my watch and marched back in with an impromptu sales pitch for it. To my astonishment, my students were riveted and stayed with me through a lesson on sales, wholesale and retail costs, and return on investment.

I had stumbled onto the truth: these kids were far more frustrated than I was. They felt so disconnected from our economic system that they saw no futures for themselves and no reason to pay attention or stay in school. Yet when I taught them business lessons, they became motivated to learn to read, write, do math, and behave better.

In 1987 I left the school system to found NFTE and bring entrepreneurship education to at-risk youth around the world. Since then, over six hundred thousand young people from Chicago to China have graduated from NFTE's entrepreneurship courses.

NFTE has developed award-winning textbooks and lesson plans that have proven successful in imparting to hundreds of thousands of students around the world free-market principles of and the mechanics of starting and operating a small business.

My work promoting entrepreneurship has taken me around the world, from New York's inner city to former communist strongholds around the world. I got to debate the labor theory of value and point out the mistakes of Marx and Lenin on a KGB-financed trip to Moscow in the dying days of the Soviet Union. Accompanied by one of the few survivors of the Khmer Rouge's bloody reign, I visited S21, a detention center in the heart of the Cambodian capital of Phnom Penh, where more than seventeen thousand enemies of the regime were tortured before being taken to the killing fields to be murdered in the service of the leadership's misguided ideology.

I have talked in prisons with inmates eager to learn the secrets of entrepreneurship, desperate to turn their lives around. I have been in the homes, offices, and workshops of budding entrepreneurs across America and the world, learning as much from them about the perils and possibilities of starting and running a business as I could ever hope to teach them.

I hope that this book will add to the critical conversation we all must have about how we can nurture an emerging global Entrepreneurship Revolution, because if it's done right, this revolution can transform the global economy and usher in a new surge in peace and prosperity, at home and abroad. Not every business succeeds; not every entrepreneurial spark lights a fire in the marketplace, but any efforts that lower business failure rates even marginally could bring a massive payoff. Any increase in entrepreneurship and business literacy will inoculate the world's people against the horrific, bloody anticapitalist revolutions we've seen develop when the poor feel disempowered, hopeless, and as frustrated as my inner-city students were before they learned that they could not only survive but thrive in the free market.

I do not use the term "revolution" lightly. My life's work has taught me the power of entrepreneurial education to change lives, to lift people up, to bring hope where none existed. And unlike the false revolutions proclaimed by prophets of the left

and right in times past, this revolution will be different in key
ways:

1. *This revolution will be truly universal.* It's hard to overstate the
amount of evil that the theories of Karl Marx have wrought, but
among his most pernicious ideas was the insistence that there
were warring classes in every society with interests that must
always be in conflict. The beauty of the Entrepreneurship Revolution is that it benefits everyone. Basic economic concepts
like the supply and demand curve were only academically for-
mulated in the last 150 years, but human beings in every society
have always had an intuitive, universal understanding of profit
and loss, buying and selling, risk and reward. Developing an
entrepreneurial ecosystem that nurtures the universal impulse
to trade will lead to an infinitely more profound "workers' revolution" than anything Marx ever conceived.

2. *This revolution will be truly democratic.* Just as the market
doesn't care where a new idea originates, it doesn't care who
came up with the idea in the first place. The people who stand to
benefit the most from a global Entrepreneurship Revolution are
the eccentrics, the overlooked, the disabled—those willing to
risk being different. To read the biographies of the great inven-
tors, the breakthrough innovators, and the founders of corporate
empires is to be struck again and again by how the outsiders
and the marginalized enjoy the greatest success in the end. The
barriers to entry they faced in nearly every other aspect in their
lives melted away in the heat of a good idea.

3. *This revolution will be truly visionary.* The entrepreneur is
a time traveler, in a sense more fantastic than any science fic-
tion story. To succeed, an entrepreneur must have the ability
to literally project him- or herself into the future, envision a
business idea as a working business, predict the potential value

of that idea, and translate that back into the present value of a product or service the business can sell in the here and now.

The global economy faces immense challenges in the coming decades. Hundreds of millions of young people will enter the labor market even as technological change threatens huge numbers of jobs and even whole industries. The wealthy nations are struggling to remain dominant, while rising economic powers in Asia, Latin America, and Africa demand their place the table. The world economy still hasn't fully recovered from the recent financial meltdown, and movements like Occupy Wall Street question the basic ideals of capitalism and free markets.

I remain an optimist because, like my student entrepreneurs, I am a time traveler, too. I can see a future where an entrepreneurial ecosystem is in place to support any young person with a good idea and the willingness to risk it in the marketplace. Not everyone is destined to be a business owner, but all can benefit from embracing the entrepreneurial mind-set in whatever job they do. The untapped potential is immense: Even in the United States, it is estimated that only six thousand high school students currently take formal courses in entrepreneurship. Why aren't we teaching our young people how our economy works? Why aren't we empowering them to participate in it?

Pablo Guzman, executive director of Foundacion and NFTE's newest international partner in Mexico City, notes that there is no shortage of entrepreneurial energy among Mexico's young people, but that far too much of it is channeled down the wrong path. He thinks entrepreneurship education programs can break the next generation of young Mexicans from the lure of quick profits and fabulous fortunes offered by the drug cartels, an attraction that is not dimmed by the rampant violence and high mortality rate of the drug trade. "They prefer five years of being rich to thirty to forty years of being poor," Guzman explains. "That's the mentality we're trying to break."

It's a mentality I have also spent a lifetime fighting. As Muhammad Yunus says, entrepreneurship is society's "great enabler," the secret weapon that can change lives and change the world. The elements in the change are financial, academic, technological, and managerial, but first, as the psychiatrists say, the patient must be willing to change. There is no greater challenge for today's political, business, cultural, and education leaders than getting this revolution right.

Steve Mariotti
New York City
April 2015

AN ENTREPRENEUR'S MANIFESTO

CHAPTER 1

Entrepreneurship Can Be Taught—to Anyone

It's a very ancient saying, But a true and honest thought, That
if you become a teacher, By your pupils you'll be taught.

—RICHARD RODGERS AND OSCAR HAMMERSTEIN,
THE KING AND I

ACCORDING TO MAPQUEST, it should take only twenty-six
minutes to travel the eight miles from the Boys and Girls
High School in Bedford-Stuyvesant, Brooklyn, to the Waldorf
Astoria on Park Avenue in Manhattan.

It took me thirty-one years, one month, and seventeen days.

I felt awestruck as I entered the Waldorf's elegant ballroom on
April 23, 2013. It was packed for a gala celebrating the Network
for Teaching Entrepreneurship's (NFTE) silver anniversary—
and I was the guest of honor. The organization I had founded in
1987 to bring entrepreneurship education to at-risk youth had
survived twenty-five bumpy yet exhilarating years. In that time
NFTE had grown from a high school teacher's pipe dream into a
nonprofit widely recognized as the leader of today's global movement in entrepreneurship education.

My first office was a wooden table at the West Fourth Street
Saloon near New York University, where I went for the free popcorn (and to nurse my crush on actress Edie Falco, who was waiting tables).

Today NFTE occupies two floors at 120 Wall Street. We have

certified fifteen hundred entrepreneurship teachers worldwide. Significant NFTE programs have been established in South Africa, Ireland, Israel, Belgium, China, the Netherlands, Germany, India, and the United Kingdom, and new programs are opening in Hebron and New Zealand. Over six hundred thousand students worldwide have graduated from our programs.

Given our humble beginnings, it was wonderful to see Goldman Sachs and MasterCard step up as the gala's primary sponsors, along with such with business all-stars as Southwest Airlines, Ernst & Young, E*Trade, Microsoft, and Sean "Diddy" Combs.

The organization has even been the subject of a movie. The documentary *Ten9Eight: Shoot for the Moon* follows teenage finalists arriving in New York City for NFTE's national business plan competition. In his January 24, 2010, op-ed for the *New York Times*, Thomas Friedman wrote, "Obama should arrange for this movie to be shown in *every* classroom in America. It is the most inspirational, heartwarming film you will ever see."

At the 2013 gala, our Global Young Entrepreneurs of the Year winners presented their businesses: Tyler Hansen had opened a paintball arcade in his Central Valley, California, hometown; Lakeisha Henderson, from East Cleveland, Ohio, had been inspired by her pet-grooming business, Besties for Life, to major in business in college; Niall Foody, age sixteen, from Letterkenny, Ireland, who has Asperger's and dyspraxia had developed an ingenious line of luminous stickers to place around keyholes, light switches, and doorbells to make them easy to find in the dark; and Abdulaziz Al-Dakhel, age eighteen, from Jeddah, Saudi Arabia, had developed a string of products from camel's milk ("a new Viagra"), wool, and even urine.

These young winners were all from challenging backgrounds.

They beautifully delivered their well-practiced pitches to the gala guests, making eye contact, shaking hands firmly, and making sure everyone who stopped by their displays left with business cards and brochures.

Later that evening, we heard from NFTE alumni like James "Jimmy Mac" McNeal, who took part in a NFTE BizCamp at Philadelphia's Wharton Business School as a high school senior in the summer of 1989. Jimmy's Bulldog Bikes became the first urban bike company in the bicycle motocross (BMX) market. Today his parent company, BDG Industries, is a major player on the BMX scene, with media, marketing, and event planning spinoffs. Jimmy remains active in NFTE as a teacher and mentor.

We also heard from Jasmine Lawrence, NFTE class of 2003. When she was eleven, Jasmine lost nearly all of her hair after using a chemical relaxer. She founded EDEN Body Works, a natural line of hair care products, and secured an order from Wal-Mart for over one hundred thousand dollars a year in sales—and her company is still growing.

AT-RISK YOUTH HAVE AN APTITUDE FOR ENTREPRENEURSHIP

These amazing young people illustrate something I have seen happen many times. Teaching at-risk youth basic business principles changes their lives—whether they become lifelong entrepreneurs or become better employees and are able to enhance their careers because they understand how business works.

I believe the biggest breakthrough of the last fifty years in education is that entrepreneurship can be taught and that it helps students in critical ways—whether they go on to become entrepreneurs or not. Young people have wonderful, unique advantages in business. As any parent of a teenager knows, they are more comfortable with risk than adults. This generation has also grown up online, watching young entrepreneurs like Mark Zuckerberg (Facebook) and Bobby Murphy and Evan Spiegel (Snapchat) turn fresh ideas into billions of dollars.

At-risk youth have additional advantages. They often display a natural aptitude for entrepreneurship because their challenging lives encourage them to develop assertiveness, independence, and salesmanship. They have a lot of experience handling risk and ambiguity. When these qualities are channeled into entrepreneurship, negative behaviors turn into positive ones. I've personally witnessed angry, disaffected, and disenfranchised children transform into creative, inspiring, empowered leaders once they've been taught how our economy works and how they can participate in it. Not only do at-risk youth exposed to entrepreneurship get excited about business, they become motivated

The entrepreneur has fascinated and frustrated theorists and researchers almost from the dawn of the study of economics. Ever since Irish-French banker and political theorist Richard Cantillon coined the term "entrepreneur" around 1730 (he also suggested "undertaker" as the English equivalent, an idea that mercifully did not catch on), economists and policymakers have been trying to pin down what makes a person an entrepreneur, how much entrepreneurs contribute to a society's growth and prosperity, and how to encourage this strange class of dreamers, risk takers, and, at times, troublemakers.

to do better in school. They realize that there are many paths out of poverty, and they discover the power of their own potential, which enhances their self-esteem.

I've made it my life's work to teach entrepreneurship education as a pathway to prosperity for at-risk youth around the world. I won't quit until every school in the world provides its students with this empowering knowledge.

LEAVING CORPORATE LIFE

This all began because, back in 1982, I wasn't a very good teacher.

Standing in front of fifty-six unruly students as a newly minted math teacher at one of New York City's most crime-ridden schools was not part of my master plan. My dreams ran more along the lines of becoming the CEO of a Fortune 500 company.

In 1977 I graduated with an MBA from the University of Michigan. During graduate school I won a scholarship to study at the Institute for Humane Studies with Friedrich A. Hayek, the 1974 Nobel Prize winner for economics.

After the summer program with Hayek I began my career at Ford. I had the best job a young MBA could get. I was an analyst for the legendary Ford finance staff.

I led a team that helped lower Ford's interest payments by several million dollars a year, earning me the nickname "Stevie Wonder." At twenty-six I was leapfrogging over career hurdles and getting an inside look at how one of America's largest corporations operated. But I soon learned that speaking one's mind did not go over well.

I was Ford's South Africa and aerospace analyst. I'd also become a fan of civil rights leader Reverend Leon Sullivan. In 1977 Reverend Sullivan drafted the Sullivan Principles. These guidelines recommended that American companies operating in South Africa under apartheid refuse to segregate their workers according to race and pay black and white workers equal pay for equal work. Sullivan, who served on the board of General Motors—the largest employer of South African blacks at the time—also lobbied American corporations to withdraw from South Africa while apartheid was still in effect.

I began corresponding with Reverend Sullivan. I disagreed with him about divestment, as it would cost black South Africans jobs, but I did raise the issue at Ford about whether we should be selling aerospace equipment to a repressive regime. I made enough of a stink that the issue reached the board of directors. Eventually Ford did change its policies in South Africa, and as international protest against apartheid grew, Ford completed a divestment agreement in 1987.

I was told that I was too controversial, and I was sacked. Burned out on corporate life I moved to New York City, thinking I might start a business. I'd always had simple little businesses when I was a kid, reselling golf balls or doing laundry. In New York I discovered that if you made products in a third-world country, it was really tough to find someone to represent you in the United States. So I started a small import-export company. Soon I was meeting interesting people from all over the world, helping them sell wood carvings and jewelry in the United States.

Being an entrepreneur had an immediate beneficial effect on my self-esteem and outlook. I was making less money, but I was my own boss. I also felt really good about helping my clients from Africa and other distant places make money and improve their lives. I loved being self-employed and started thinking about expanding into other ventures.

But then I learned another life lesson—about living in a large city.

A Life-Changing Jog

One lovely fall afternoon in 1981 I set out for a jog along the East River. I passed a group of teenage boys lounging against the railing that ran along the riverfront.

"Get him," one of them said.

They roughed me up and took the ten-dollar bill I had in my running shorts. They waved knives in my face, shoved me around, and taunted me. My hands were trembling. I couldn't believe this was happening in broad daylight.

After knocking me to the ground, they sauntered off. Dazed, I got to my feet and blinked in the bright afternoon sun. No one seemed to have noticed a thing. I stumbled out of East River Park and made my way toward home. On the way, I ran into a group of policemen. They took me to their station to file a report.

Afterward, the entrepreneur in me wondered why these kids would risk prison for ten dollars. If they had been able to sell me something or ask me to invest in a business, they could have gotten a lot more money. That would have been a win/win situation for everyone.

After the mugging I developed flashbacks and nightmares. I was diagnosed with post-traumatic stress disorder by a therapist who suggested I confront my new fear of teenagers by becoming a teacher. My mother had been a beloved special-education teacher back in Michigan, so the idea actually appealed to me.

I had also been told I should become a teacher by Ayn Rand, although perhaps she was being sarcastic. I knew the great writer in her final years, and we talked at length about the power of free markets and the wonders of capitalism. One day she turned to me and said, "Steve, you talk too much. You should be a teacher."

Back then, New York City had a serious teacher shortage. Basically, if you had a college degree and seemed reasonably sane, they'd let you teach. I told the school board that I wanted to teach in the most troubled schools and work with the most difficult children. The school board was happy to oblige.

A Breakthrough Born of Desperation

In 1982 I was assigned to Boys and Girls High School in Bedford-Stuyvesant, Brooklyn. Boys and Girls had established itself as the most dangerous school in the nation. The student dropout rate was 70 percent. Seventy-two teachers simply refused to report for duty—they preferred to be unemployed. In 1978 the New York State Board of Regents took the unprecedented step of putting the entire school on probation.

My students were incredibly rowdy, and I had no idea how to quiet down my classrooms enough to even try to teach. On March 6, 1982, I was attempting yet again to teach a class at Boys and Girls High School. The day before, someone had set a coat on fire in the class. This day wasn't going any better. Frustrated and close to tears, I stepped out into the hallway to try to gather my composure. The kids didn't even notice that I was gone.

I racked my mind for answers. I had been bored and inattentive in high school, too. What had interested me? Money. I always had some little business going. Earning money was always what had interested me most. It was probably the only reason I had ever bothered to learn to read, write, or do math.

I whipped off my watch and marched back in to the classroom. I held it up and screamed over the din, "Hey! What is this worth?"

You could hear a pin drop, and, as if by magic, I became a teacher.

Tyrone, one of the most troublesome kids, said clearly: "I would pay twenty-five. Nice watch, Mr. Mariotti."

Another echoed him, "I would go twenty."

Suddenly, the class was debating the value of my watch, so I pushed them: "Where does the store buy it from?"

If the first question began my career, the second made it last a lifetime. The secrets of buying goods from a wholesaler in bulk and selling individual pieces at higher prices to make a profit poured out of me, and my students were fascinated. The next day I brought in a wrench, and we discussed the distribution chain that runs from manufacturer to wholesaler to retailer, with profit markups for every link in the chain.

Soon we were calculating gross and net profit and return on investment. We discussed business cycles, investing, present and future value, marketing, and more. I was teaching my students supply and demand, how prices communicate information, and Austrian trade cycle theory—and they were getting it!

Entrepreneurship Education Motivates Kids to Learn

Out of sheer desperation I had discovered something magical. Entrepreneurship can be taught, even to the most disruptive kids in the worst high schools in the country. *Especially* to them. They know how to hustle, they understand the value of a dollar, and they long to participate in our market economy—but they have no idea how. That is often the source of their frustration and acting out. In too many neighborhoods, the only people teaching our youth entrepreneurship are drug dealers. That has to change.

I came up with business-based games to motivate my students to learn math. I had students make change in a role-playing retailer/customer scenario, for example. The retailer had to make ten correct transactions—or lose the turn if he or she made a mistake. Nobody wanted to make a mistake.

This game treated math as a practical reality rather than an abstraction. More subtly, it gave the retailer a chance to experience ownership. What had begun as intuition slowly developed into a certainty: Whenever I could focus a lesson on business, I had my students' attention.

I began using all my ingenuity to teach the bedrock principles of entrepreneurship: buy low/sell high, keep good records, and satisfy a consumer need. When these young people grew interested in business, they wanted to know how to add, subtract, and divide so that they could calculate their rates of return. They wanted to be able to read and write and speak more effectively.

I also had students make mock sales calls. This game taught them that to sell they had to be civil and polite. They had to convince customers to buy from them; they could not coerce or bully (or mug!) them.

I found *The Wall Street Journal* to be a valuable teaching tool. I used it to hold stock contests: Each kid would pick a stock and track it. The holder of the stock that gained the most in six weeks would earn a prize. The students quickly learned to read the stock tables, and I pointed out that the CEOs of America's largest companies—and indeed everybody who was anybody in the business world—were reading, that morning, that very same newspaper. One class became so obsessed with *The Wall Street Journal* that I ended up supplying each student with a daily copy at my own expense.

During the 1980s, I spent eight thousand hours in the classroom developing lessons using entrepreneurship to motivate young people to learn to read, write, and do math. I ran school stores and used them as entrepreneurship labs. Above all, I taught my students the power of ownership to transform their lives. I proved to them that they could participate in our economy. The sky was their limit. They were not doomed to live on welfare, or to risk their lives and freedom selling drugs. Armed with this knowledge, many of my kids started successful little businesses, developed bigger businesses, went to college, landed good jobs, and helped their families and communities.

Teaching Ownership to At-Risk Youth Changes Their Lives

In 1987 I left the New York City school system to found NFTE and devote my life to bringing entrepreneurship education to at-risk youth around the world as a pathway out of poverty.

To be honest, I left because I was frustrated in my efforts to promote business literacy within the school system. I was repeatedly warned by supervisors not to talk about money in the classroom. In addition, the grip that the United Federation of Teachers enjoyed hurt not only students and taxpayers, but also teachers by removing any incentive to try new ideas or take initiative. In the end, although I loved teaching, I felt I could help more children by devoting myself full time to my new mission.

Slowly, NFTE started to gain recognition. The sight of inner-city kids running businesses was a great story for the media. ABC News and other programs came running to do profiles.

Despite the good press, however, NFTE was by no means an overnight success. Every day was a financial struggle in the early years.

NFTE did not invent formal entrepreneurial education, and we certainly weren't the only ones out there providing it. But we had a single-minded focus on bringing entrepreneurship education to at-risk high school students, and that was key to our success. Not every business leader I pitched agreed to become a donor, but all of them grasped the importance of our mission.

Sometimes even those who refused to donate inadvertently let me know I was on the right path. I ran into some wealthy people whose attitudes toward teaching poor children about business formation and ownership were pretty shocking.

One day I met with one of the owners of one of the country's top private equity firms. He was very philanthropic and had sponsored scholarships for many young people—but he balked at donating to NFTE.

I didn't understand this. I said, "You're doing so much for education by putting deserving students in private schools. Why don't you spend some of that money to also teach them how to become business owners?"

A tall, imposing man, he let his glasses slide down the bridge of his nose and looked warmly, yet quizzically, at me, like an uncle indulging a favorite nephew. As if it were the most obvious, rational statement in the world, he said, "But, Steve, then who would do the work?"

I wish I could say that was the only time I ever heard this. Sadly, I've heard variations of this argument from a wide range of wealthy and powerful people.

Owners have enormous power in the world, and he knew that. Children raised in poverty are typically not thinking about who owns the stores in their neighborhood or the buildings in which their families rent apartments. They are not taught that ownership is a craft that can be learned.

I started to realize that entrepreneurship education does more than just teach at-risk kids some business skills. It changes what they believe is possible for their futures.

We were showing our students more than just how to make some money. They were discovering that life is not a hierarchy and we don't live in a class system. Just because they were living in poverty didn't mean they had to stay on welfare or work dead-end jobs for their entire lives.

If you believed that was your future, working your way up the ladder in a drug-dealing gang might look pretty attractive to you, too.

RESEARCH PROVES RESULTS

Today, NFTE's award-winning high-school curriculum is used in hundreds of schools. We have partnered with Brandeis University and Harvard University to conduct the first-ever studies of the effect of entrepreneurship education on at-risk youth. These studies prove that students exposed to entrepreneurship education programs develop new aspirations, longer time horizons, and greater self-esteem. Our anecdotal evidence and data both indicate that entrepreneurship education motivates teens to stay in school, increases their interest in college, makes them better employees, builds their confidence and self-esteem, and raises their business formation rates.

Research by the Harvard Graduate School of Education found that high-school students who took a fifty-hour entrepreneurial course showed increased interest in furthering education and career aspirations, increased feelings of control over their lives, and increased leadership behaviors.

NFTE research findings further indicate that these entrepreneurial courses increase engagement in school, increase students' sense of connection with adults in business and the community, increase independent reading, and increase business and entrepreneurial knowledge.

Entrepreneurship Education Lengthens Time Horizons

I noticed while teaching, and research has confirmed, that learning about entrepreneurship helps students become more comfortable with delayed gratification. It lengthens their time horizons.

Poor people tend to deal in very short time preferences. It's hard to save money if you are barely covering rent, utilities, and groceries. Five years of big money as a drug runner starts to look like a good career move. Blowing any extra money you do have on drugs or other diversions that make you feel better seems like a good idea when you feel hopelessly trapped in poverty.

In NFTE programs we take students on two field trips. The first is to a wholesale district. The students receive fifty-dollar grants, which they may use to purchase goods from wholesalers. A week later, we take the students to sell their wholesale goods at a flea market—typically marking them up 100 percent, or "keystoning." They create flyers and signs to market their goods at the flea market, and they must keep track of their inventory. After the flea market, they are required to prepare simple income statements and calculate their gross and net profit.

For many of these kids, this is a magical moment. If they have successfully held onto to their wholesale products long enough to sell them at the flea market, if they've chosen products that appeal to their customers, and if they didn't blow the fifty dollars on gifts for themselves, they go home with one hundred dollars. This opens a teen's mind to the benefits of delaying gratification and the power of "buy low, sell high." Our pre- and post-tests of children who complete NFTE programs consistently show a lengthening of their time horizons as a direct result of these kinds of experiences.

Savings Represent Confidence in the Future

The entrepreneur needs these longer time horizons. He or she must be a time traveler, able to spot a consumer need, and imagine filling it in the future and creating a profitable business. The entrepreneur sacrifices time, energy, and money in the present in order to create a more profitable future.

Savings and investment are just money's way of time traveling as well. Savings are an expression of confidence in the future. When we save, we create capital.

At NFTE we are obsessive about imparting the value of saving. Every student receives a savings account in order to save capital to execute his or her business idea. Students are required to deposit at least 10 percent of their profits from the flea market and other selling events into their savings account.

We make it easy to accumulate capital, but hard to spend it: Students must write a one-page memo that the teacher must sign before any withdrawals from savings are approved. We post signs around the classroom on the value of savings and hold games to see who can build up the biggest nest egg.

It was easy to explain the role of money as a medium of exchange to my students: I give you ten dollars and you give me a pizza. It was much trickier to explain to them the value of saving that ten dollars and delaying the gratification of eating that pizza. But as they learned how to make money from money, they grasped the many ways they could build up capital. They learned that investing in one's reputation, education, and network of customers and mentors are all ways to accumulate capital and improve one's future.

Entrepreneurship Education Helps People Handle Change

Perhaps my most disruptive students took to entrepreneurship like ducks to water because entrepreneurship is all about disruption! The great Austrian American economist Joseph Schumpeter first identified the socially profitable disruption that entrepreneurs can wreak. The railroads, for example, put a string of once-profitable stagecoach companies out of business. Netflix pioneered a way to deliver entertainment to homes, and Blockbuster went out of business.

English-born U.S. economist Israel Kirzner further refined Schumpeter's work by demonstrating that entrepreneurs provide key signals to the economy about misallocated resources by seeking out and exploiting high-profit niches.

A major argument for entrepreneurship education is that it helps people become more nimble and able to handle the stresses and anxieties of change. In NFTE programs we do many exercises that help students learn to roll with the fact that markets are constantly changing. They learn that a savvy entrepreneur can always adjust and make money. Students are given scenarios such as the following: "What would happen if gasoline prices doubled? How can you make money?" They throw out all kinds of interesting ideas. If you were there, you would be very impressed with their energy and creativity.

Imagine the innovation and creativity that would be unleashed if everyone in the world grew up with an education in entrepreneurship and was familiar with the idea that change is the only real constant. Imagine if everyone had the basic business skills to respond to change with confidence and to create new opportunities in the face of losing a job.

We need the Entrepreneurship Revolution because entrepreneurship education helps people overcome challenges, build sustainable development, create jobs, generate renewed economic growth, and advance human welfare.

Entrepreneurship Education Tackles Dropout Rates

In the United States, our 1.2 million high-school dropouts cost over $329 billion in lost wages annually, according to the Alliance for Excellent Education, founded by former West Virginia governor Bob Wise.

The decision to drop out is a one-million-dollar decision in lost wages for each child who makes it. Furthermore, 90 percent of the fastest-growing employment categories in America require a college degree—and dropouts won't be able to compete for them.

In *The Silent Epidemic*, author John Bridgeland interviewed high-school dropouts and asked them why they dropped out of school. Eighty-one percent said they would not have dropped out if classroom subjects were more relevant to their lives.

How to make it financially and how to own their futures as economically productive members of society are relevant lessons that motivate youth to stay in school. Entrepreneurship education engages young people and inspires them to go to school. It teaches them skills they can apply to improve their lives. Bringing business leaders into classrooms to share their expertise and optimism connects students to their communities and gives them mentors and networking opportunities.

In President Obama's March 10, 2014, State of the Union address, he directly addressed reforming the No Child Left Behind Act and bringing entrepreneurship into our classrooms: "I am calling on our nation's governors and state education chiefs to develop standards and assessments that don't simply measure whether students can fill in a bubble on a test, but whether they possess twenty-first-century skills like problem-solving and critical thinking, entrepreneurship and creativity."

We can't afford to let 1.2 million young Americans fail annually. We need to fast-track the Entrepreneurship Revolution so that we do not lose another generation of students before we can teach them to fuel their dreams and believe in their own potential.

A Lost Generation Threatens
Global Stability

It's not only American dropouts who threaten the U.S. economy. In her article "Bachelor Bomb," *Quartz* editor Gwynn Guilford notes that Bank of America / Merrill Lynch research cites a huge global male youth boom as a serious source of more market turmoil and global instability. By 2030, three out of five people living in cities will be under the age of eighteen.

A close relationship exists between surging populations of underemployed young men and revolutions, wars, terrorism, and other upheavals. The Bank of America / Merrill Lynch analysts cite the English Revolution (1642–51), the French Revolution of 1789, and the emergence of the Nazi party in the 1930s in Germany as historic examples.

The idea that entrepreneurship education could be key to eradicating poverty, crime, and violence is gaining momentum. In January 2010 I spoke at the Davos World Economic Forum about the critical importance of providing entrepreneurship education to all children around the world. The Forum's Global Education Initiative has adopted this as one of its two goals, along with ensuring that every child graduates from high school.

When there aren't enough jobs to employ young men, they have less to lose by banding together and committing crimes, or even joining terrorist organizations. This situation is becoming acute in China and India, where a cultural preference for boy children has resulted in many more young men than young women. In China, the spread between males and females in the twenty-to-forty-nine age bracket will blow past 20 million in 2015. India currently has about 17 million more young men than young women.

Unemployment is a key factor motivating young Muslims to join radical groups like al Qaeda and ISIL, as Iftlin Foundation executive director Mohamed Ali noted in a 2013 TED talk. Ali described frustrated young people like the 70 percent unemployed in his hometown of Mogadishu, Somalia as living in "waithood"; waiting for some way, anyway to move forward with their lives. "Waithood," he explained is "a gateway to terrorism," but "entrepreneurship can be the most powerful tool against waithood," because it "empowers young people to be the creators of the very economic opportunities they're desperately seeking."

EMPACT 100—Young Entrepreneurs Doing It for Themselves

Throughout this book I report on the latest Entrepreneurship Revolution efforts around the globe. One exciting initiative is EMPACT 100, a networking event for America's top young entrepreneurs under age thirty-five held in New York City. This invite-only collaborative gathering introduces the most influential leaders in the youth entrepreneurship ecosystem to top government, education, media, foundation, and corporate leaders.

EMPACT 100 is run by NFTE alumni Michael Simmons and Sheena Lindahl. Their company, Empact, also runs the Extreme Entrepreneurship Tour, which brings young entrepreneurs to colleges to speak.

Featured EMPACT 100 delegates in 2014 included Kay Koplovits, founder of the Sci-Fi Channel and Springboard, an innovative organization that helps women find venture capital; Jeff Hoffman, philanthropist and founder of Priceline; and Chip Paucek, CEO of 2U and Hooked on Phonics. What an incredible opportunity for the invited young entrepreneurs to network with heavyweights who can help them take their businesses to the next level!

I asked Sheena to tell me more about EMPACT 100 and the future of youth entrepreneurship.

STEVE MARIOTTI: What is the vision behind the Empact 100 Showcase?

SHEENA LINDHAL: Our goal is to celebrate the stories and faces of young entrepreneurs. We do this by selecting entrepreneurs thirty-five and younger from companies that have made at least one hundred thousand dollars. We focus on a variety of areas where entrepreneurs succeed. This ensures that the EMPACT

100 aren't just from the tech industry or super high-growth companies, but represent a real range of this country's young entrepreneurs.

SM: Do you think entrepreneurship among young people is on the rise?
SL: I think entrepreneurship is starting to be seen as a more viable career path. In part, this may be because safe, stable career paths of previous generations have proven in recent years to be less secure in the long run. I think the perception of entrepreneurs is still skewed toward those individuals involved in the tech industry—people getting multimillion-dollar investments right at the start. This stands in contrast to countless entrepreneurs who are bootstrapping and working their companies from the ground up outside the tech industry. These businesses may be flying under the radar but are nonetheless growing into successful businesses.

This is why we are trying to show the many faces of entrepreneurship. Not everyone has the personality of Richard Branson or a business model like Mark Zuckerberg's. One type of entrepreneur is not more entrepreneurial than another.

I have observed a deep hunger for entrepreneurship education around the world. The economic winners in this new century will be those countries that harness and nurture the entrepreneurial drive that is innate in all human beings.

In the words of Daniel Isenberg, founder of the Babson Entrepreneurship Ecosystem Project and a recent adviser to the Obama administration's Startup America initiative, "I've come to believe that entrepreneurship is part of the human experience. It's like art, literature, music, and poetry. I think that is beautiful, even though I may or may not be an entrepreneur."

I believe young people around the world have a right to entrepreneurship education. Every individual has the right to be exposed to ownership concepts, the possibility of ownership, and the principles that lead to capital accumulation and wealth creation. These rights are grounded in the individual's entitlement to ownership of his or her labor, time, resources, and ideas.

CHAPTER 2

Nurturing the Entrepreneurial Mind-Set

Business opportunities are like buses, there's always
another one coming.

—RICHARD BRANSON

A S NOTED in the previous chapter, youth unemployment is one
of the most destabilizing problems in the world. Certainly,
when unemployment hit 9 percent in the United States during
the global financial crisis that began in 2008, it was frightening.
But did you know that the teen unemployment rate during that
time was over 25 percent? The rate among African American
teens rose to almost 49 percent, and the rate for Hispanic youth
went to 35 percent. Youth unemployment rates have also been
extremely high in Europe, leading to costly, disruptive rioting in
the streets of London, Athens, and other cities. The Entrepreneurship Revolution must bring entrepreneurship education to
our youth worldwide in order to reduce these catastrophic youth
unemployment rates. Without such initiative, we risk losing this
generation to long-term structural unemployment.

I don't believe our low-income teenagers lack initiative or
don't want to work. I believe many do not know how to create opportunities for themselves because they have not been
exposed to the tools and ideas necessary to create ownership
of assets within the free enterprise system. Our schools do not
teach them how our economic system works, and their parents
may not know how to teach them either.

Professor Andrew Hahn of Brandeis University has noted the social consequences for an entire generation brought up in poverty that has never set foot in a workplace and the potential benefits of entrepreneurship education. Hahn notes, "Research studies show the scarring effects of early unemployment. The lack of work experience among minority teens contributes to a host of more serious challenges in their early twenties. Studies demonstrate that NFTE's entrepreneurship programs are among the few strategies that work during these periods of massive youth joblessness."

Entrepreneurship education makes young people more employable and also teaches them that they can create jobs for themselves. They learn that they do not have to be victims of their circumstances or an economic downturn. They learn to recognize opportunities even during tough times.

The Entrepreneurial Mind-Set

What is it about exposure to entrepreneurship that changes the psyche so positively? What is the entrepreneurial mind-set, and how can we encourage it?

The *Financial Times* defines the entrepreneurial mind-set as "a specific state of mind which orientates human conduct towards entrepreneurial activities and outcomes. Individuals with entrepreneurial mind-sets are often drawn to opportunities, innovation, and new value creation. Characteristics include the ability to take calculated risks and accept the realities of change and uncertainty."

In *The Entrepreneurial Mindset: Strategies for Continuously Creating Opportunity in an Age of Uncertainty*, authors Rita Gunther McGrath and Ian MacMillan define the entrepreneurial mind-set as combining confidence in one's own judgment with a ruthless focus on cultivating what works and jettisoning what doesn't.

"In a world of uncertainty, our guiding philosophy is: Take Charge," they write. "If nobody knows what the future will hold, your vision to navigate it is as good as anyone's. The future may well belong to you."

"Entrepreneurs don't see barriers," notes Elizabeth Gore, the first-ever "resident entrepreneur" at the United Nations Foundation and the chairwoman of the UN Foundation's Global Entrepreneurs Council. "To an entrepreneur, barriers are merely challenges that you climb over, slip under, go around, or push through."

The challenge that the Entrepreneurship Revolution poses is this: How do we make the entrepreneurial mind-set more accessible worldwide? We can do this by exposing our youth to concepts like ownership, free markets, and comparative advantage and giving them opportunities to explore their own comparative advantages and develop them into small businesses.

At its heart, creating the entrepreneurial mind-set is an exercise in consciousness raising. Ultimately we are all always in business for ourselves, with our primary asset being our future time and how we spend it. But are we aware of that fact?

People in poverty don't typically think about who owns the corner store or the building in which they live. They are not taught that ownership is an achievable craft or that they have unique knowledge that can be turned into a business. But that can be changed.

The earlier the entrepreneurial mind-set is introduced in our young people, the more potent it can be. Start teaching young people to observe the needs of others and to think about how to satisfy those needs through voluntary trade and make a profit. When you see a store, discuss it. Point out prices. Point out quality. Raise their consciousness about ownership. Ask them who owns that building? What would that building sell for? How could we get money to buy that building? What problems does our community have? What new businesses would solve them?

According to the National Center for Children Living in Poverty (NCCP), as of 2014 more than 16 million children in the United States—22 percent of all children—live in families with incomes below the federal poverty level, which is $23,550 a year for a family of four.

The NCCP notes that, on average, families need an income of about twice that level to cover basic expenses. Using this standard, 45 percent of America's children live in low-income families. Entrepreneurship education can improve this dismal statistic.

Entrepreneurship Education Makes Youth More Employable

Entrepreneurship education makes young people more employable because they learn how business works. They begin to "get" what makes an employee valuable. This shift in viewpoint toward the entrepreneurial mind-set can immeasurably benefit the psyche of unemployed teenagers, and it also benefits companies that hire them. Imagine how you would react if a young person came to your office looking for a job and she knew how to read an income statement—or if he could calculate return on investment and understood the economics of one unit.

Currently, our national strategy to combat poverty among low-income youth revolves around improving K–12 education. Yet we're not teaching entrepreneurship or financial literacy, even though most Americans would probably agree with President Obama's statement during his American Jobs Act speech to Congress: "Everyone here knows that small business is where jobs begin."

WE MUST ALSO TEACH OUR YOUTH THE POWER OF OWNERSHIP

Currently, our national education efforts are focused on teaching low-income youth to become better workers. Given the widening wealth gap in the United States, however, why aren't we also teaching them how to own? If entrepreneurship is the engine of the U.S. economy, why aren't we raising more owner-entrepreneurs?

This is how fortunes and jobs are created: An entrepreneur starts a business, sells some or all of its ownership, and uses the resulting capital to start and build other businesses to sell in the future to create even more capital. Workers, on the other hand, spend their lives selling only their time for hourly wages, or perhaps a salary.

Teaching business skills without also teaching ownership potentially creates wealth for an owner down the line, not necessarily for the entrepreneur who created the business. Even well-educated entrepreneurs can find themselves at a disadvantage when dealing with venture capitalists and other professional owners who are experts at obtaining equity and a high rate of return in exchange for investing in a business.

If only the wealthiest people own the increased profits resulting from the better education of our low-income youth, how much has really been accomplished in helping our most impoverished citizens achieve the American Dream? How can we expect the wealth gap, which movements like Occupy Wall Street are protesting, to improve?

LET'S DEMYSTIFY WEALTH CREATION

Entrepreneurship education programs must teach not only record keeping, sales, finance, negotiations, opportunity recognition, and marketing—but also the power of ownership. Students must learn to value and sell a business and build wealth with franchising, licensing, and other ownership advantages. Entrepreneurship education demystifies wealth creation for our low-income students, giving them the same knowledge that a child of wealthy parents might pick up at the dinner table. Entrepreneurship education empowers young people by teaching them that every individual has five assets: time, talent, attitude, energy, and unique knowledge of their communities. They learn to use these assets strategically to find paths out of poverty.

THE WILLIAMS BROTHERS

I'd like to share with you the story of two at-risk youth who were saved by entrepreneurship education. Jabious and Anthony Williams were living with their mom and eight other family members, crammed into their aunt's two-bedroom apartment in Anacostia, a violent southeast Washington, DC, neighborhood. Every day the boys walked miles to the nearest Exxon station to pump gas for tips. "Typically, we would earn about thirty to fifty dollars a day to help support my mom," says Jabious Williams.

At Suitland High School in Maryland, the Williams brothers met Mena Lofland, a NFTE-certified business teacher. She got the boys in to her entrepreneurship class. Like many of our low-income students, Jabious and Anthony displayed an aptitude for entrepreneurship, born of tough childhoods that encourage independence, toughness, salesmanship, and hard-won street smarts. I've seen this repeatedly: Our at-risk youth are uniquely equipped to handle the risk and uncertainty inherent in entrepreneurship. They also have valuable insights into their local markets.

The Williams brothers started their own hip-hop clothing line with support from Lofland and two local mentors—Phil McNeil, managing partner of Farragut Capital Partners, and Patty Alper, a dedicated volunteer, philanthropist, and former entrepreneur. The brothers knew what kinds of clothes their friends would buy, and their line was a local hit. Their success gave them the confidence and the funds to help their mother and build their futures.

Jabious went to Southeastern University on a scholarship, and today he operates Jabious Bam Williams Art & Photography Company. Anthony heads a youth mentorship program. They gave their mom five thousand dollars as a down payment for a house. "If it weren't for the NFTE classes and the support of our teachers and mentors, we would have been likely to drop out of school," Jabious notes.

The story of the Williams brothers is just one of countless examples from NFTE's files that beg the question: If entrepreneurship education can create jobs, prevent students from dropping out, and provide economic rescue for people in our low-income communities, why isn't it standard in every high school in America?

Entrepreneurship education can help solve the youth unemployment crisis, rescue our low-income communities by increasing home ownership and employment, and even bring about a fairer distribution of wealth without government intervention. We need a national debate on owner-entrepreneurship education, particularly for low-income youth. We must raise the consciousness of those who have been left out of our economic system so that they comprehend the joys and responsibilities of ownership and have the tools and mindset to compete and succeed.

As Williams says, "Because I own my business, I know I have a future."

FIGHTING UNEMPLOYMENT IN FRANCE

Unemployment has proven to be a dangerously destabilizing force in Europe, and France is no exception. Over the last decade the country has experienced a series of youth riots that have shaken its societal foundations. The 2005 riots were the most serious and most widespread—leading to the declaration of a national state of emergency—but smaller riots such as the August 2012 Amiens uprising in northern France illustrate what can happen when youth and police clash.

At the height of the confrontation, 150 officers—local and federal riot police—faced off against young men who fired buckshot and fireworks at them. Unemployment skews higher in northern France and among the country's youth. Two weeks prior, the French government declared Amiens among fifteen impoverished zones that would receive more money and security, but clearly the city's youth were still frustrated at what they perceived as official indifference to their plight.

With 150,000 young people dropping out of school annually without a degree, many fear that the 2014 youth unemployment rate of 25.4 percent in France will continue to rise. This raises the possibility that more frustrated unemployed youth may turn to violent extremism, such as the deadly January 7, 2015 attack at the offices of the satirical newspaper, *Charlie Hebdo*.

In December 2013 I flew to Paris for the inaugural business plan competition of Réseau Étincelle, the umbrella group running NFTE programs in France, led by Sylvain Breuzard and Lena Bondue (cofounder of NFTE Belgium), who, with Olivier Vigneron, has cofounded the French youth entrepreneurship movement. Vigneron is our top entrepreneurship teacher in France, and Breuzard is CEO of the successful French consulting and information technology firm Norsys.

I attended the presentation of wonderful business plans by ten French entrepreneurship students. Their businesses included gardening, painting, and repair services. The judges asked intense questions, and the young presenters answered with poise and obvious pride in their creations. They understood their markets, and they nailed their financial statements.

After the presentations I talked with the students. One said he "was creating a business in order to help with the unemployment problem in Europe." I was touched by his motivation. An immigrant from the Middle East, he lived in the suburbs of Paris, where the unemployment problem among youth, particularly minorities, is very apparent.

"Are you optimistic about the future?" I asked. "Yes, I am," he replied, showing me the logo he had created for his business and explaining his economics of one unit in great detail.

NFTE has also established NFTE Belgium and NFTE Germany, and we are running programs in Ireland, Austria, and England with various partners.

THE GRIT SCALE

I have been particularly struck by the brilliant work of University of Pennsylvania researcher Angela Duckworth, a 2013

MacArthur "Genius Grant" recipient. Dr. Duckworth argues that the essential quality of the entrepreneurial mind-set can be summed up in what she calls, simply, "grit."

Duckworth has developed a Grit Scale to measure her subjects' ability to stick to an interest or goal over the long term—a critical attribute for any successful entrepreneur. Half the questions on the test seek to measure the subject's ability to work hard and respond "resiliently" in the face of failure or an unexpected setback. The other part of the test measures a candidate's ability to sustain consistent interests—what she calls "focused passions"—over a long time. Grit, she argues, "is not just having resilience in the face of failure, but also having deep commitments that you remain loyal to over many years."

In her TED talk, Dr. Duckworth said, "One characteristic emerged as a significant predictor of success. It wasn't social intelligence. It wasn't good looks, physical health, and it wasn't IQ. It was grit. Grit is a passion and perseverance for very long-term goals. Grit is stamina. . . . Grit is living life like it's a marathon and not a sprint."

Asked how a culture can build up grit, she replied, "I don't know," adding, "What I do know is that talent doesn't equal grit. There are many talented individuals who simply do not follow through on their commitments.

"Don't believe failure is a permanent condition," Dr. Duckworth argued. "We need to be gritty about getting our kids grittier."

Entrepreneurship Encourages Grit

One good way to get our kids grittier is to expose them to entrepreneurship and encourage them to try starting their own little business. The earlier we can get our youth comfortable with evaluating risk and reward, with discovering their own strengths and abilities through the roller-coaster ride of starting and operating a small business, the better.

Nina Burrowes, a British psychologist who studies the psyche of the entrepreneur, has noted that it takes an unusual and especially strong character to become a successful entrepreneur. "If your experience of being an entrepreneur includes moments of vulnerability, doubt, guilt, fear, and anxiety," Dr. Burrowes says, "the good news is—you're doing it right. It should feel like this. Why? Because many of the challenges that entrepreneurs face tap into some of the core psychological challenges that we all face."

We Are All Entrepreneurs

Resiliency and flexibility are emerging as key twenty-first-century virtues. Supporting an entrepreneurial personality should be one of the primary goals of education at all levels. We are all entrepreneurs in the sense that we all sell our time, and we all must learn to bounce back from failure and adapt rapidly to change. Entrepreneurship education helps our young people become more comfortable with change and more nimble at adapting to it.

My hometown of Flint, Michigan, was once synonymous with lifelong jobs that are rare today. You could go to work for General Motors after high school or college and fully expect to stay there, earning a comfortable living for your family and then enjoying a secure retirement. Times have changed. According to the Bureau of Labor Statistics, Americans born between 1957 and 1964 held an average of eleven jobs between ages eighteen and forty-four. The velocity of job changes for Millennials (born between 1977 and 1997) is expected to be far higher.

Job hopping is the new normal. Ninety-one percent of

Millennials expect to stay in a job for less than three years, according to the Future Workplace "Multiple Generations @ Work" survey of 1,189 employees and 150 managers. That means they will have fifteen to twenty jobs over the course of their working lives.

Career counselors speak of the need for developing one's own "brand." Even workers on traditional job paths must embrace a more entrepreneurial mind-set. Donna M. De Carolis, dean of the Charles D. Close School of Entrepreneurship at Drexel University, argues that modern life and the new global economy are forcing us to expand the idea of entrepreneurship itself, and that the mind-set it takes to start a business will become increasingly valuable to all career paths.

"When we choose to embark on a path not charted, we are engaging in a 'small act of entrepreneurship,'" De Carolis wrote in *Forbes*. "Being entrepreneurial is essentially about thinking and doing something that we have not done before, in order to achieve a desirable goal or outcome. It is about assessing a situation, designing alternatives, and choosing a new way—or perhaps a combination of ways—that we hope will lead us to something better, however we happen to define 'better' at that moment.

"We are selling ourselves short if we do not define ourselves as entrepreneurs," Carolis added. "If we choose to accept that 'entrepreneurs' are the 'other' people who take a chance, who think and act differently when challenges arise."

How Does a Nation's Culture Affect Entrepreneurial Mind-Set?

I've spent my life teaching kids whom society has written off, and I am certain there is no entrepreneurial gene that only a favored few have. I believe that anyone can develop an entrepreneurial mind-set. International surveys do, however, show clear differences in national attitudes toward starting a business, the social prestige of ownership, and the stigma of business failure.

Entrepreneurship "is a complex endeavor carried out by people living in specific cultural and social conditions," according to the 2012 Global Entrepreneurship Monitor (GEM) report, the biggest comparative study of entrepreneurship across cultures and countries ever conducted. GEM notes:

> The positive or negative perceptions that society has about entrepreneurship can strongly influence the motivations of people to enter entrepreneurship. Societies benefit from people who are able to recognized valuable business opportunities and who perceive they have the required skills to exploit them. If the economy in general has a positive attitude towards entrepreneurship, this can generate cultural and social support, financial and business assistance, and networking benefits that will encourage and facilitate potential and existing entrepreneurs.

One cultural aspect that entrepreneurship experts track is societal attitudes toward failure. "Failure," as Henry Ford famously said, "is simply the opportunity to begin again, this time more intelligently." That is the attitude entrepreneurs must cultivate toward failure in order to succeed.

Why, then, according to a GEM survey of nearly seventy countries, do Uganda and Zambia score higher on nearly every measure of favorability to entrepreneurship than global industrial powers like the United States, Germany, and Japan?

Some 81 percent of Ugandans polled by GEM researchers said

Gayle B. Jagel, CEO at the Young Entrepreneurs Academy, which provides entrepreneurial education programs targeting middle-school and high-school students, notes that social media success stories have had the unintended consequence of making life harder for the next generation of business risk takers.

Facebook, Twitter, and the rest are "great," she says, "but they can be awful at the same time. Now if you're a young person who tries something and comes up short, it's all out there. It's on Facebook, it's on YouTube. We have to be able to say, 'It's OK to fail.' Some of the greatest successes in the business world followed a lot of quiet failures. We have to remove that stigma, because failure is always going to be part of the equation."

they saw entrepreneurial opportunities in their economy, and just 15 percent cited "fear of failure" as one factor holding them back. In the United States, which is generally cited as the most entrepreneur-friendly economy in the developed world, only 43 percent of those surveyed reported seeing entrepreneurial opportunities (and just 13 percent said they were considering starting a business), and the fear of failure rate is 32 percent, twice that in Uganda.

The measures of enthusiasm for entrepreneurship in Japan, which is still the world's third biggest economy and home to a slew of world-class manufacturing and high-tech companies, are even lower. Just 6 percent of Japanese respondents said they saw economic opportunity for business start-ups in their country, and only 2 percent expressed an interest in going into business for themselves—the lowest rates of any country polled. Some 53 percent cited business failure as an inhibiting factor, the highest level in the world after Italy (58 percent). The numbers may reflect cultural and economic biases in Japan, as well as the strain of the country's "Lost Decade" of economic stagnation since the 1990s.

GEM researchers caution against drawing a straight line between entrepreneurial enthusiasm and economic success, though. Japan is obviously richer than Uganda and will be for many decades to come. Although Zambians express high levels of support for starting a new business, the country reports an "established business ownership rate" for those start-ups of just 4 percent, half the U.S. average and less than a third the rate for other sub-Saharan African countries.

Despite having "the highest entrepreneurship rate across the entire sample, [Zambia] has less than one-tenth this level of established business owners, leaving questions about why so many people are entering entrepreneurship while there are rarely any running businesses beyond these early stages," the GEM researchers observe. In other words, having citizens with the drive to start a business is a necessary—but far from sufficient—prerequisite for building an enduring entrepreneurial society. The ability to forgive and learn from business failure is key as well.

Are Mature Economies Going Soft on Risk?

The Amway Global Entrepreneurship Report, released in late 2013 by the U.S. Chamber of Commerce, found that cultural attitudes toward failure and bankruptcy have a noticeable impact on an economy's dynamism. Would-be entrepreneurs in some countries, GEM found, demand a much higher level of certainty before taking the plunge: "Countries that show a high fear of failure are also the ones that long for 'low-risk business models.' In Germany (34 percent) and Italy (29 percent), 'low risk' is among the top three factors that encourage entrepreneurship. . . . The cultural attitude toward uncertainty also bears a strong influence on the risk assessment as a reason against self-employment."

The European Commission's Competitiveness Council in late 2012 concluded in a report that it is "essential for the EU to put in place an environment which helps entrepreneurs take risks and start new businesses. Failed entrepreneurs remain entrepreneurs, and are a precious resource. Due to experience gained by repeat entrepreneurs the failure rates of second start-up attempts are lower than for initial efforts. We should therefore support entrepreneurs and give them a second chance."

The numbers suggest the entrepreneurship challenge is particularly acute on the continent. A September 2013 GEM youth entrepreneurship study, conducted with the nonprofit group Youth Business International, found that just 17.3 percent of young Europeans believe that good business opportunities are available and that they have the skills and resources to exploit them. That compares to 60 percent in sub-Saharan Africa, 40 percent in Latin America, and 30 percent in the Middle East and North Africa.

Youth Business International CEO Andrew Davenport said the findings strongly suggest that too many young people everywhere "have the will, but not the means" to start a business, but the problem is particularly acute in Europe.

"It's worrying that whilst many young people do see good

opportunities for starting up a business, most of those in Europe do not," he said. "At a time when we need more new businesses to help drive our economy forward, we want people to come together to support and encourage entrepreneurship in any way they can."

According to GEM, U.S. entrepreneurs report the lowest rates of fear of failure in the developed world. Just 31 percent of American adults reported that they would be dissuaded from starting a business because of the possible stigma of failure. This attitude has been one of the United States' prime comparative advantages. That statistic has been creeping up in recent years, however, possibly as a by-product of the Great Recession.

In a widely discussed 2013 article, *The Wall Street Journal* posited that a "risk-averse culture" has "infected" the United States. "Three long-running trends," the *Journal* piece noted, "suggest the U.S. economy has turned soft on risk: Companies add jobs more slowly, even in good times. Investors put less money into new ventures. And, more broadly, Americans start fewer businesses and are less inclined to change jobs or move for new opportunities."

GLOBALLY, MANY PEOPLE ARE BETTER OFF

New studies have also exploded some myths regarding capitalism. Instead of creating a permanent class of winners and losers, the global Entrepreneurship Revolution is already transforming the lives of billions of people in broad swaths of Asia, Eastern Europe, Latin America, and Africa.

The Penn World Table, created by the Center for International Comparisons at the University of Pennsylvania, is the most ambitious database ever compiled to measure the relative size of the global economy. When the latest update was released in July 2013, much of the media coverage focused on who was moving up and who was moving down. When would China's GDP surpass the United States'? Which Asian tiger was winning the race? Which emerging market would be the next market darling, and which countries seemed stuck at the bottom of the heap?

But step back from the horserace comparisons, and a far brighter picture emerges. My belief that the Entrepreneurship Revolution will usher in an unprecedented era of growth and prosperity rests on how incredibly far the world's economies have already come in the last half-century. The Penn World Table proves that the collapse of Soviet communism and embrace of free-market practices (if not ideals) by once-socialist governments around the world has, in statistical terms, led to a larger increase in income and living standards for billions of people than the average Briton saw at the height of the Industrial Revolution.

GDP in the Philippines and Zimbabwe, for example, grew faster between 1960 and 2010 than did GDP in the United Kingdom between 1820 and 1870. According to the Penn data, in 2010, 3.5 billion people—half the world's population—lived in countries with an average per capita GDP of six thousand dollars or more. That may not sound like much, until you realize it is roughly equal to the per capita GDP of Italy in 1960.

Charles Kenny, a fellow at the Center for Global Development and the New America Foundation, puts the Penn World Table data in perspective:

> Around 5.1 billion people live in countries where we
> know incomes have more than doubled since 1960,
> and 4.1 billion—well more than half the planet—live

in countries where average incomes have tripled or more. Nearly 2.2 billion people are in countries where average incomes have more than quintupled over the past 50 years. This includes the citizens of China, Japan, Egypt, and Thailand—all of whom have seen around an eightfold increase in average incomes since 1960.

The larger point, says Kenny, is that the market has proved the pessimists wrong when it comes to culture and economic growth. Although billions around the world still live in poverty, the Penn World Table research confirms "that traditional Malthusian fears of national output constrained by resources have absolutely no basis in reality anywhere. They also suggest that concerns over widespread 'poverty traps'—where countries are condemned to penury and stagnation by centuries-old institutions or culture or genetics—are more a figment of economic theorists' imaginations than a major factor in real-world economic outcomes." Culture, it would seem, is no barrier to prosperity in any country that gets its economic policies and incentives right.

SURPRISING ENTREPRENEURIAL ACTIVITY IN THE POOREST ECONOMIES

The 2012 GEM report found an unexpected entrepreneurial ferment in some of the world's poorest economies: The entrepreneurial landscape of sub-Saharan Africa "is changing rapidly, and the region is now becoming a mecca for business development and growth," according to Mike Herrington, a professor at South Africa's University of Cape Town and lead author of the report on the region. "Opportunities abound, and a positive spirit is emerging amongst the population of these countries," Herrington noted.

According to the regional survey, the ten sub-Saharan economies—Angola, Botswana, Ethiopia, Ghana, Malawi, Namibia, Nigeria, South Africa, Uganda, and Zambia—are "in the midst of an entrepreneurial revolution that is invigorating the region with new opportunities, increased employment, and a robust rise in gross domestic product to one of the highest GDP growth rates in the world." Africa's real GDP rose by nearly 5 percent from 2000 to 2008, double that of the previous two decades, even as the local economies became less reliant on traditional mining and agricultural operations. Outside investment, and particularly outside private investment, as opposed to government aid transfers have boomed in recent years, although these were set back for a couple of years by the global recession.

"Entrepreneurs in the sub-Saharan nations have among the highest entrepreneurship rates in the world, with women participating at equal or nearly equal rates in most of the countries we studied in this region," said study coauthor Donna J. Kelley, who teaches entrepreneurship at Babson College. "This shows an incredible ability for people here to create their own jobs, and in many cases, jobs for others. As a result, entrepreneurship in sub-Saharan Africa can contribute substantially toward providing income for families and lifting communities out of poverty."

In March 2014 *Marie Claire* magazine published "Continental Shift: Women Techies Abound in Africa's Silicon Savannah" by Dayo Olopade. Olopade documented an exciting flurry of female-led tech entrepreneurship in Nairobi's Bishop Magua Centre, ground zero for tech start-ups in Kenya.

AkiraChix, for example, is an all-female collective of self-proclaimed geeks who founded the group in 2010 to encourage more Kenyan women to enter the burgeoning African tech industry. AkiraChix founders Marie Githinji, age twenty-nine; Judith Owigar, twenty-eight; Linda Kamau, twenty-seven; and Agenal Odur, twenty-five, have developed exciting products like iMatch, a tool that helps nongovernmental organizations orchestrate the flow of charitable goods so that they actually meet local needs, and a magnifying app for visually impaired computer users. The collective also teaches entrepreneurship, coding, and programming classes to young women.

Bright China: Teaching Entrepreneurship to Chinese Youth

One of NFTE's greatest successes has been in China, where we have partnered with Bright China Foundation (BCF). So far, we've reached over 14,000 students annually with more than 350 trained instructors. BCF's programs stretch beyond Beijing and Shanghai, bringing entrepreneurship education to Heilongjiang, Guangzhou, Sichuan, and Yunnan provinces as well.

Bright China serves the country's vocational education system as well as prison inmates and lower-income students. BCF's annual National Business Plan Competition is a major event in the country—covered on the national news! I am repeatedly blown away by the quality and ingenuity of the business proposals that BCF's young entrepreneurs bring to the competition. If there's a culture barrier for China's young entrepreneurs, I have not seen it.

Lisa Miller, an NFTE staff member who worked with inner-city American public and charter schools after getting her MBA from Columbia University, shared her impressions of NFTE's

Chinese partnership after a recent visit. She said the Chinese students took the competition extremely seriously, often offering finished, ready-to-market products and services. "It was clear that running their own business was much more than exercise for these students," Lisa reported. "They had chosen it as a serious option for their future and were embracing it with fervor, many already running profitable businesses."

Experiencing the power of the entrepreneurial idea in a different culture was, Lisa adds, "nothing short of amazing. I was immediately struck by the camaraderie of the student competitors. Each student had assistance from fellow competitors, many of whom were meeting each other for the first time, in setting up their presentations and showcasing products before the audience and judges. It was incredibly refreshing to see them be so supportive of each other while simultaneously competing to be awarded the winning prize."

Lisa added that she was humbled by the earnestness with which Bright China embraced its partnership with NFTE, clearly articulating that it has given thousands of students across China who previously had limited options an alternate choice. These students in China are like so many other children across the world battling poverty, unemployment, and low expectations reinforced by so many factors beyond their control. They have reinforced in my mind that entrepreneurship education provides a path around these obstacles.

The Entrepreneurial Mind-Set and the Middle Class

China's economic growth proves the value of unleashing the natural entrepreneurial energy of tens of millions of ordinary citizens who are now free to start businesses. China and India are both rapidly creating new middle classes that are bigger than the entire population of the United States. In turn, the United States must nurture its next generation of entrepreneur or it will continue to experience slow growth and a shrinking middle class. We can use entrepreneurship education to get all our students— even the most disenfranchised—excited about their future. If we help them become financially literate, and arm them with business knowledge, they will contribute to our nation's growth.

KidZania

KidZania is a remarkable business education program for children that does just that. KidZania is the brainchild of Xavier López Ancona, an educational genius and entrepreneur who lives in Mexico City. KidZania is a miniature city designed to teach financial literacy to children ages four to sixteen. Over twenty million people have visited KidZania since he opened his first location in Mexico City in September 1999. Today, there are nearly a dozen KidZania locations in North and South America, Europe, Asia, and the Middle East. If you care anything about kids and entrepreneurship, schedule a visit and prepare to be blown away.

In these fantastically rich microcities, parents cannot go into the stores—in order to keep the atmosphere of play strong and "just for kids." Visiting kids get bracelets that let parents know exactly where they are at any moment via a remote viewing device. This also helps KidZania collect data on which "stores" the child enters and what he or she buys. There are safety precautions and cameras everywhere. Parents can visit a spa, business center, or beauty salon.

I needed special guest privileges to be on the floor, as this is typically a kids-only environment. I saw thousands of kids working, buying, marketing, and browsing, and on their faces was the intellectual glow of experiential education at its best. All of the facilities are constructed to 70 percent of their actual size to make kids feel grown-up. (Being only five feet five myself, I felt right at home.)

The entire place is run and patronized by kids. Trained adult "Zupervisors" are available to help children complete their tasks, but the kids are really running the show. KidZania locations have their own currencies, flags, holidays, and national monuments, and a Declaration of Independence that concludes, "Get ready for a better world!"

This is an unrivaled example of an experiential program in the field of work, job training, and financial literacy—one that has taken education to a higher level by making it immersive and fun. In Mexico City's KidZania, you will find eighty-two branded stores familiar to adults. The children are assigned age-appropriate jobs so that they can earn the local currency, "Kidzos." In fact, when you arrive at KidZania, the first thing you do is open up a savings account. You get a debit card and can withdraw Kidzos or save them for future visits. Kidzo currency is honored worldwide at every KidZania location.

In addition to stores, there are ambulances, police cars, and miniature trucks—all driven by the children executing the civic duties of a real city. There are mock fires, and the child-run fire department is dispatched to put out the "fire." There is a medical lab, an oil well, and a day-care center. I grew hungry as we visited the restaurants—Italian, Japanese, and Mexican kiosks. There is a supermarket, a cookie factory, a cereal factory, a cosmetics factory, and, most incredible of all to my mind, a crime-scene investigation school. The aviation center was fascinating, as was the driving school. One young boy remarked to me, "I wish this was my full-time school," and I agreed. I wanted to go to school here full time for a year so that I could learn about all the different job trainings for kids.

Visitors go through "customs" as they cross the border into the official state of KidZania. The next stop is the job placement service Manpower, where I took an aptitude test. Turns out I am very artistic! I received my résumé and was given a set of businesses for which I showed an aptitude, from working at the acting academy to attending cooking school. I also was assigned to the schools that taught driving and gardening and was encouraged to go to the global education center, perhaps proving I made the right decision years ago by becoming a teacher.

I walked with wonder through the sports stadium and yogurt manufacturing company. I was guided through the natural disasters training institute, where children were learning how to react in a flood. There is a radio station, a theater where kids produce and act in their own plays, a moving company, a police station, a tax office, and even a court complete with kid lawyers and judges.

Everything is designed with exquisite attention to detail. When a simulated fire breaks out, the firefighters use state-of-the-art hoses and spray water to put it out. The coins made in the central bank are driven in a van to the retail banking outlets accompanied by police guards in uniform. A sports gym and a gas station are managed solely by the children.

This wonderful city teaches entrepreneurship and ownership experientially by mixing fun with genuine accountability. It is one of the most exciting approaches to entrepreneurship education I have ever seen. Children also learn history through statues scattered throughout the cities of such greats as Mahatma Gandhi and the pioneering printer Johannes Gutenberg.

López Ancona told me, "KidZania teaches children the skills they need to be independent." I think he is a pioneering genius, and his work needs to be replicated all over the world. There are twelve sites globally—the latest just opened in Bangkok, with another nine in the planning stages. López Ancona also plans to open numerous sites in the United States.

Each park is geographically tailored to the needs and culture of the city where it is based, and activities are sponsored by corporate brands known in that market. "The thing I most like about KidZania is really that we're empowering kids to be better citizens," López Ancona added.

CHAPTER 3

Who Are the World's Entrepreneurs?

W HAT CAN BE done to foster more business creation around the globe? Before we can explore that question, we need to answer a few others: Who are the world's entrepreneurs? In which countries do they thrive? Are they mostly men? Women? How do they get funding? What is their attitude toward risk?

What follows is a survey of the latest international research on entrepreneurship. By exploring this data, a clearer picture emerges of what's working to promote business creation, what needs to be done, and where the areas of greatest need lie.

GLOBAL ENTREPRENEURSHIP BAROMETER

Ernst & Young regularly puts out an "Entrepreneurship Barometer" measuring how the Group of 20 (G20) nations—the United States and its leading industrial partners, plus such rising powers as China, Brazil, and Turkey—are faring in the promotion of entrepreneurship in their economies. The report examines five "pillars" that affect the quality of a nation's environment for entrepreneurs: access to funding, entrepreneurial culture, taxes and regulations, coordinated support between government and economy, and entrepreneurship education.

The results are based on interviews with some fifteen hundred new business owners across the G20, along with statistical and policy comparisons and more in-depth interviews with roughly 250 entrepreneurs, academics, and experts in the field.

The bottom line: No country has a monopoly on wisdom when it comes to creating a positive atmosphere for entrepreneurs. Every country has strengths and weaknesses.

In the 2013 survey the United States came in first in two of the five pillars, receiving top marks on access to funding for entrepreneurs and entrepreneurial culture. The United States was also rated third behind only France and Australia on the quality of its entrepreneurship education and training.

The United States ranked thirteenth, however, on the quality of its tax and regulation regime, while low-tax Saudi Arabia topped that list. The United States came in dead last in what the survey calls the "coordinated support" that a country's government and its economy offer to entrepreneurs.

A Wake-Up Call for the United States

That last result, the Ernst & Young report notes, is a "wake-up call" for those who think the United States is the most entrepreneurial nation in the world. "In what might come as a shock to many," the report states, "the United States performs poorly in terms of its coordinated support, including networks, mentors, and incubators, for entrepreneurs. . . . While the U.S. may have a well-developed support network in place, many entrepreneurs still feel more support is needed.

"The weakest results were in relation to official programs and agencies," the report continued. "Only 9 percent of entrepreneurs surveyed in the U.S. say that access to government start-up programs has improved, compared to 32 percent across the G20."

No country scored in the top five in every category. Saudi Arabia's favorable tax and regulatory structure for entrepreneurs hasn't translated into a dynamic private sector for the kingdom, for example, because its oil-dominated economy has made it hard for new small businesses to find their footing. Indeed, Saudi Arabia scores in the bottom half on every other standard measured in the survey.

The Ernst & Young report concluded, "There is a huge scope for countries to make improvements across the board in their entrepreneurial ecosystems, but one area in particular emerges as a priority. According to the entrepreneurs themselves, access to funding is the single area where improvements are most urgently needed. Seven out of ten entrepreneurs in our survey say it is difficult to obtain financing in their countries."

The report also cautioned that countries should "avoid looking at problems in isolation; instead countries need to understand how the five pillars interrelate. Countries need to focus not only on individual pillars in their ecosystem, but also on providing coordinated support across all these vital areas."

Inside Saudi Arabia

When I hear that a conservative, male-dominated, devoutly Muslim oil sheikhdom cannot support entrepreneurship, I think of Muneera Al-Maneeam, the young Saudi girl from Riyadh who was one of NFTE's Global Young Entrepreneurs of 2013, an annual contest in which NFTE participants from around the United States and the world pitch their start-up ideas to business professionals. Muneera was one of two Saudi finalists in the international competition that year, which included entrants from China, India, Ireland, and Chile.

Dust, Muneera observed, is a big problem in arid Saudi Arabia, but there are no good commercial scales on the market that could calibrate the exact amount of dust in the air.

"In our environment, measuring dust is a necessity, because it's around us most times of the year. Dust is a health issue, especially for children," Muneera explained during her business plan presentation.

With some technical help from her father and uncle, Muneera fashioned her own dust scale using the same standards that are employed to measure fog. The first entrepreneur in her family, she expressed deep gratitude for their support. "Proving myself and being trusted by others is the biggest reward I've had so far," she told me.

Muneera's example convinces me that the coming revolution in entrepreneurship in some ways has barely begun. While the United States, Europe, and Japan struggle to revive the entrepreneurial spark in their mature economies, for much of the globe the transformations that entrepreneurship can achieve are just getting under way!

Males Still Lead the Entrepreneurship Pack

Although Muneera's story is encouraging, and even though some of the most successful and inspiring graduates of NFTE programs have been young women, a 2013 Amway Global Entrepreneurship Report that surveyed two dozen countries found that the "average" entrepreneur is still predominately young, university educated, and male.

The Amway Report found that, on average, men express a greater entrepreneurial ambition than women by a 44 percent to 33 percent margin. The gap between the sexes actually widened two percentage points compared to a similar study conducted the previous year. The differences were particularly stark in Italy, where 52 percent of Italian males said they considered starting their own business at some point in their lives, compared to just 32 percent of Italian women.

Interestingly, the United States has consistently ranked number-one among seventeen countries surveyed regarding conditions that foster high potential female entrepreneurship, according to the Gender-Global Entrepreneurship Development Index (GEDI). These conditions include entrepreneurial environment, entrepreneurial ecosystem, and entrepreneurial aspirations.

THE EDUCATION GAP

The Amway Report also uncovered a persistent education gap when it comes to entrepreneurial ambition. Even though legendary dropouts like Ted Turner, Ralph Lauren, Bill Gates, and Michael Dell have created business empires, the survey found that while 82 percent of those with a college degree or higher express a belief in their ability to strike out on their own, only 67 percent of those without a college degree felt confident about trying entrepreneurship.

In addition, the survey noted that "entrepreneurship education is seen as an encouraging factor by many more graduates than by respondents with no degree," adding, "Therefore policymakers should consider already incorporating entrepreneurship education in school education to foster an entrepreneurial culture."

ENTREPRENEURS MAY VALUE INDEPENDENCE MOST

When fourteen- to twenty-nine-year-olds were asked in the Amway survey which aspects of entrepreneurship appealed to them, the most cited factor was "independence from an employer / being my own boss" at 48 percent, up from 43 percent in the previous poll. That was followed by "self-fulfillment / realize my own ideas"—45 percent; second-income prospects—30 percent; better home / work / leisure time balance—26 percent; and returning to the job market—18 percent. This was one category in which America's youth stood out, with a chart-topping 65 percent saying they considered starting their own company as a way to be their own bosses.

This result backs up what my decades in the classroom have taught me: personal autonomy, not money, is often the primary motivation that gets someone fired up to start a business.

What Factors Make Entrepreneurs Successful?

The Kauffman Foundation for Entrepreneurship has conducted one of the most systematic studies ever of five-hundred-plus successful company founders, asking them what was critical to their survival in the earliest days and what factors contributed to their present success. The group surveyed included successful executives in fields ranging from aerospace and defense to computers, health care, and services. For most, the survey showed, money and connections rated well below experience and drive as factors in success.

"The responses to this survey clearly contradict some strongly held beliefs about starting a business and entrepreneurship," the researchers wrote. "The four most important factors for entrepreneurial success, according to our respondents, are prior work experience, learning from successes and failures, management teams, and luck."

Financing Not as Crucial Early On

Many of the entrepreneurs surveyed said that networking and obtaining financing were important, but not as crucial as one might believe, to their early successes.

The Kauffman study reports, "Few took venture capital or angel financing in their first ventures. The lesser role of venture capital funding implied by the responses indicates that perhaps this avenue of funding is less useful for first-time entrepreneurs than even bank funding. Further, the lack of importance that entrepreneurs place on investor advice implies that they value 'smart money' less than expected, and that entrepreneurs are even more self-reliant than previously assumed."

Asked to cite the biggest deterrent to entrepreneurial success, 98 percent of the business executives cited lack of willingness to take risks. Even the entrepreneurs who succeeded, the researchers noted, "considered entrepreneurship to be a risky endeavor."

Although strong majorities cited the benefits of professional networks (70 percent) and a university education (70 percent, rising to 86 percent for Ivy League graduates), the other factors noted received even higher scores. Ninety-six percent of the surveyed entrepreneurs said prior work experience was important, while 88 percent said being able to learn from both success and failure is critical.

Global Differences in Fear of Failure

More surprises come from one of the most extensive international surveys on entrepreneurial attitudes ever conducted. The Amway 2013 Report polled some twenty-six thousand respondents in the United States and twenty-three other developed countries. The results vividly dramatized a common frustration for those of us who have made promoting entrepreneurship our life's work: Positive attitudes toward entrepreneurship far out-run the number of people willing to take the plunge and start their own business.

The two opposing factors hit with virtually equal force. According to the Amway survey, 70 percent reported having a positive attitude toward entrepreneurship, while exactly 70 per-cent also cited "fear of failure" as the strongest obstacle holding them back from trying self-employment. Striking differences exist across borders and cultures; the United States' 37 percent "fear of failure" rate in this survey is the lowest in the industrial world, while Japan's is the highest at 94 percent.

The report grouped the consequences of failure into three cat-egories—social, psychological, and financial—and noted, "The fear of financial consequences of business failure is an obstacle to becoming self-employed (41 percent). Social consequences such as disappointing family, friends, and coworkers and psy-chological consequences like personal disappointment all rank far behind financial consequences."

"You can't separate entrepreneurship from risk taking," noted John Raidt, a scholar at the U.S. Chamber of Commerce Founda-tion and a senior fellow at the Atlantic Council. "But you need a society that values agility. When it is deployed in force, entre-preneurship can really be one of the most successful weapons in our arsenal."

How the Global Recession Affected Global Entrepreneurship—OECD Survey

In one sense, however, all recent research paints a somewhat inaccurate picture of the state of entrepreneurship in today's global economy. The global recession has likely skewed the statistics by obscuring positive trends that were slowed by the economic downturn. Joblessness remains a major problem in countries across the globe. Companies old and new are still struggling to regain the momentum lost since the 2008 financial crisis.

The Organisation for Economic Co-operation and Development (OECD), in its "Entrepreneurship at a Glance" survey, found that business start-up rates "remain below the pre-crisis levels, particularly in the euro area," while the share of "high-growth companies"—typically the start-ups and maturing young companies that provide an economy with much of its dynamism—fell to between 2 to 4 percent in 2010, the worst year of the downturn. That's half the 3.5 to 6 percent range seen in virtually all OECD countries in 2006, before the worldwide economy tanked.

"The recent crisis, characterized by tighter credit restrictions, has arguably hampered new start-ups and impeded growth in existing start-ups, as well as their ability to survive in tough market conditions," the OECD report states, adding, "The significant rise in business closures, especially of micro and small enterprises, in recent years bears stark witness to these difficult conditions and highlights the need for statistics on entrepreneurship that can support policymakers."

Luckily this is already a picture drawn from a rearview mirror. The frozen credit pipelines of the global economy are slowly thawing, and business profits—if not business investment— are returning to precrisis levels. The world's entrepreneurs are regaining their footing. They face new challenges and opportunities in education, technology, finance, and governance. The challenge is to put the data we now have to productive use, to plot the best path from where we are now to where we want to be.

Why Are Entrepreneurs Important to the Global Economy?

I have built my career on the belief that anyone can benefit from learning how to start and maintain a small business. I believe that increasing the number of entrepreneurs in our world will reverberate on a grand scale by helping to grow the global economy and decrease—or even one day eliminate—poverty. I think most of my colleagues in the entrepreneurship education movement would agree, but we could stand to be more conversant in the theoretical underpinnings of our movement.

I spoke with one of America's top economists and entrepreneurship education advocates, Peter Klein, in order to gain insight into the larger question: Why are entrepreneurs important to the global economy? Klein is a professor at the University of Missouri and research fellow at the Mises Institute, where he focuses on entrepreneurship, organization, and business strategy. He is an Austrian economist, meaning he belongs to the Austrian school of economic theory, which believes that the subjective choices of individuals underlie all economic phenomena. Austrian economists seek to understand the observed economy by examining the social ramifications of such individual choice.

STEVE MARIOTTI: Why is entrepreneurship important?
PETER KLEIN: The terms "entrepreneur" and "entrepreneurship" are used in many different ways, and not always consistently. Typically people mean a specific kind of business, like a

start-up company, a small company, or a high-growth company. But we also use the word "entrepreneurial" to describe a particular kind of thinking—being creative, showing initiative, being alert to opportunities, exercising responsibility.

Following the American economist Frank Knight and the Austrian Ludwig von Mises, I think that the entrepreneur peers into the uncertain future, trying to judge what goods and services consumers will want, and trying to meet those demands by investing in the present. This responsibility is held by all business owners, as they try to make a profit by creating economic value. Entrepreneurial judgment is essential to a market economy—it's what creates and sustains firms, introduces and develops new technologies, brings untold benefits to ordinary people, and underlies all the creative genius of a market economy. Start-ups require judgment, of course, but judgment is about more than just start-ups or high-tech companies.

SM: What can a government do to promote entrepreneurship?
PK: Government officials talk about giving us more and better entrepreneurship, but what they usually do is pick particular firms, industries, or technologies they like and give those firms subsidies and other benefits. There is nothing inherently wrong with having more of these kinds of firms, but the market should decide which firms, and which types of firms, succeed and fail. What entrepreneurs need is secure property rights, the rule of law, and sound money. The best thing government can do for entrepreneurs is get out of their way.

SM: Are there particular government policies that hurt entrepreneurship?
PK: Our current monetary regime, with hyperactive central

banks that create booms and busts, creates a terrible climate for entrepreneurs. Artificially low interest rates distort market incentives, leading to what Ludwig von Mises and Friedrich Hayek called "malinvestment." Taxes and regulations make it harder to start and to run companies, favor some companies at the expense of others, and hamper bargaining between firms, financiers, employees, and customers. Think of the uncertainty caused by the Affordable Care Act or the heavy reporting burdens imposed by Dodd-Frank.

Mises wrote that in an economy such as ours, where the state plays a huge role in all aspects of business, entrepreneurship degenerates into "bribery and diplomacy." Instead of focusing on creating value for customers, entrepreneurs spend their time lobbying for favors or to avoid penalties, trying to discern the government's next move, and anticipating or adapting to the newest regulations.

SM: What should low-income countries and communities do to increase the rate of business formation?

PK: Same as wealthier countries and communities: Don't constrain entrepreneurs with bad policies, but don't try to subsidize them either. Let the market sort it out. Of course, start-ups and self-employment are important for economic growth, but they aren't necessarily superior to large enterprise and other forms of commercial activity.

SM: There are globally over three hundred million unemployed young people. Do you think entrepreneurship can help create the jobs of the future?

PK: Absolutely! Entrepreneurship—in the broad sense of responsible stewardship over productive resources—is what makes a market economy tick. A healthy, entrepreneurial economy is the best solution to unemployment and the remedy for broader social problems as well.

PIONEERING NEW ENTREPRENEURIAL ECOSYSTEMS

Increasingly, governments are getting the message: Entrepreneurs are key to improving every nation's economic health, wealth distribution, and even political stability. But will they listen to Peter Klein's recommendations or stand in the way?

Some government efforts are afoot that do seem to be on the right track. The United States has named business formation and the support of new entrepreneurial efforts as prime goals of its economic policy. Israel has generated a robust venture capital and entrepreneurship sector by promoting immigration; building private-sector incubators; aligning research institutions, the military, and entrepreneurs; and highlighting entrepreneurship in schools across the country. South Korea and Japan have both announced ambitious programs to spark new entrepreneurial energy in their economies, and the government program to create an entrepreneurial ecosystem in Austria—not usually seen as a global pioneer in such matters—is among the most impressive I've ever seen.

SOUTH KOREA'S "CREATIVE ECONOMY"

An interesting national experiment in fostering a positive entrepreneurial ecosystem is under way in South Korea. The country is already a star performer in the global economic sweepstakes, building a modern, export-led, high-income economy out of the ashes of a devastating civil war. The country's famed *chaebols*—global brands such as Hyundai, Samsung, LG Group, and Hanjin—have helped fuel spectacular growth rates. In the most recent Ernst & Young survey, South Korea's entrepreneurship culture ranked second among all G20 nations, behind only the United States.

The South Korean government has embarked on a closely watched coordinated campaign to improve its national infrastructure and support for entrepreneurs that is unmatched in the world. For all its success, South Korea faces the same hurdles to entrepreneurship as other countries: dominance of the market by older, established firms; an education system that stresses cooperation and established patterns of learning over creativity; red-tape bureaucracy; and a preference from Korean parents for their children to work for established companies. "If you start a business and fail, that failure sticker will be with you for the rest of your life," Daniel Shin, founder of TicketMonster, South Korea's largest shopping-discount website, told Bloomberg Markets.

South Korea's first female president Park Geun-hye is determined to change all that with a "Creative Economy" initiative to foster a new appreciation for small businesses and entrepreneurship. "The past economic model designed to catch up with advanced economies drove Korea's rapid growth, but it has lost steam," President Park Geun-hye says. Her agenda includes a comprehensive set of tax incentives and regulatory reforms intended to address financing challenges for start-up firms that will foster a "virtuous cycle" of funding and investment for start-ups akin to Silicon Valley. Other measures include increasing public investment in basic research by 40 percent by 2017, expanding government procurement opportunities for start-ups, supporting promising new sectors and initiatives, and promoting entrepreneurship through education and public outreach.

The effort faces considerable skepticism, but President Park has set aside nearly $3 billion in funding for start-ups, with another $89 million for "bounce-back" entrepreneurs looking to start over after a failure.

New Efforts in Japan

Japan is also making new efforts to encourage entrepreneurship since recognizing that its cultural bias in favor of "salary men" was causing growth to stagnate. The relative dearth of opportunity-driven entrepreneurship has contributed to the nation's economic malaise over the past two decades—since the asset price bubble burst in 1991.

As Yoshito Hori argued in an influential *Japan Today* article, "Fostering an Eco-System for Entrepreneurs to Promote Growth" (November 8, 2011), "We need to nurture a set of new values and a culture where entrepreneurs who have succeeded behave in a manner that will lead society to view them as role models. As a result, their risk taking will be showered with praise."

Hori, managing partner at GLOBIS Capital Partners added,

> We should aim to create a set of values and culture that affirms that the most outstanding members of society should take the risk and aspire to create new businesses. If we succeed in doing this, everyone will naturally start to think about entrepreneurship and launching new businesses. In turn, this will lead to

the creation of new value in society and the emergence of a vibrant and dynamic society. Ultimately, this will encourage the shift of human resources, capital, knowledge, and other valuable resources to new industries.

Data from the OECD Science, Technology, and Industry Scoreboard reveals that, both in absolute terms and relative to GDP, Japan has been trailing the other OECD countries in the annual amount of venture capital invested. The Global Entrepreneurship Monitor found that only 1.9 percent of people in Japan between the ages of eighteen and sixty-four are working actively to establish new businesses, compared to 4.9 percent of U.S. adults.

Meanwhile, an in-depth analysis of Japan's economic woes by two Japanese professors, called the Fukao-Kwon Report, revealed that from 1996 to 2006—when total employment in Japan decreased by 3.5 million—young, newly established firms and foreign companies were the only ones to create net job growth. Japan was lagging other developed nations in entrepreneurship and looking at flat GDP projections. It wasn't hard to connect the dots.

In 2012 the United States and Japan launched a bilateral U.S.–Japan Innovation and Entrepreneurship Council comprising government and private-sector leaders to explore how to better encourage entrepreneurship in both countries. The Council concluded that Japan needs to build a better entrepreneurial ecosystem.

According to Jonathan Ortman's insightful article "Japan's Entrepreneurial Imperative" in the 2014 Entrepreneurship.org newsletter,

The good news is that there is already a cacophony of local startup communities in Japan populated by smart, global, open, socially motivated founders driven to do good and do well. Impact Japan has done an outstanding job with the Honda Foundation of seeding a next wave of startup fever, of the like felt at Startup Weekend, TEDx, and Japan Satellite events in Tokyo and elsewhere in Japan. Today, we cannot talk about Japan's entrepreneurship ecosystem without mentioning Open Network Lab ("Onlab"), a startup incubator equivalent to a Y Combinator or TechStars in the U.S., which has already provided three batches of startups with mentorship, office space, and a suitably small amount of cash in exchange for a piece of equity.

Onlab's director, Hiro Maeda, noted in an interview with TechCrunch's Brenden Mulligan in 2011 ("Startup Japan"),

Launching a startup, where there is a lot of uncertainty and unsuitability, does not fit a culture where harmony and stability are strongly emphasized. However, a lot of younger Japanese are realizing that the nation itself is at a point of uncertainty. The employment rate of college graduates has reached the lowest point in the past decade, and the Japanese earthquake has made the people in the entire nation uncertain about their future. The uncertainty and the increasing interest in the success that Silicon Valley is experiencing has made more younger Japanese take bigger risks.

ARE WOMEN THE FUTURE OF ENTREPRENEURSHIP?

Interestingly, Japanese female entrepreneurs constitute one of Japan's fastest-growing economic sectors. Some experts have speculated that Japanese women may wind up taking the lead in Japanese entrepreneurship because they do not face the intense pressure that Japanese males do to seek long-term corporate employment and support their families.

The role of women in Japan's economy is gathering momentum as the country seeks to jump-start its economy. Some eight hundred working women gathered for the seventeenth International Conference for Women in Business in Tokyo in July 2012, and their message was clear: Japan needs to tap female innovation if it wants to experience the rapid economic growth happening in other parts of Asia.

As I mentioned previously, Austria has done a lot to encourage entrepreneurship—and focusing on women has been a big part of that. Since 1997 the percentage of Austrian female start-ups has increased by 13 percent. In 2010, 30,673 people established an enterprise; 53.2 percent were women. In the same year, about 38.7 percent of all Austrian enterprises were managed by women. This growth is a direct result of special programs targeting women, including a special training program for "female-led microbusinesses" begun in 2006 that provides training and coaching.

In 2010 Austria's Women in Business organization launched a management-prep program, Female Future, to encourage more women to explore senior management and serve on advisory boards and boards of directors. Women in Business has also successfully demanded tax deductions for home help for child care and *Betriebshilfe* (business continuation aid), which provides a qualified replacement for an entrepreneur who is temporarily unavailable (due to maternity leave for example), so that her business will not suffer.

Female Entrepreneurs Help Restore Cambodia

Perhaps no nation on earth has been more decimated by communism in recent years than Cambodia. It's impossible to travel through Cambodia without being deeply moved and horrified by the genocide that the Khmer Rouge inflicted upon Cambodians from 1975 to 1979. Roughly 1.7 million citizens, or one in four, were murdered as Khmer Rouge leaders pursued their insane vision of a communist utopia. Entrepreneurs were among the groups targeted for extermination. Business owners were routinely murdered and their assets seized.

On January 7, 1979, the Vietnamese government overthrew the Khmer Rouge, which retreated to the northern forests of Cambodia. They left behind a grievously wounded country that is still recovering from their genocidal rampage.

On my 2013 trip to Cambodia, however, I was profoundly moved by the entrepreneurial, never-give-up spirit of the people. Just thirty-eight years after the communist holocaust, Cambodians are embracing business. I was amazed by how warmly I was greeted by senior government dignitaries and entrepreneurs alike. I spent nearly two weeks walking the streets of different villages and cities and met eager entrepreneurs everywhere I went. They are revitalizing Cambodia and helping it recover.

Female entrepreneurs are playing a major role in rebuilding the Cambodian economy. I met with many of the women pioneering this effort at a lunch with the Cambodian Women Entrepreneurs Association (CWE). The CWE has about 150 female entrepreneurs in its membership, and its mission is to help women build their own companies.

CWE was founded by Pok Nanda and the managing director of Sentosa Silk, Seng Takaknery. Nanda's other pursuits include political coaching; she trains young women to run for office. Thirty years ago, there were no women in local Cambodian government; now there are eight. In the national parliament, women account for 18 percent of the membership, and they were all trained by her organization, Women for Prosperity.

At the lunch meeting, I spoke with Lim Popna, who told me about her travel and tourism business. Lee Banny also presented her company, a profitable jewelry shop. Chenda Clias described what it is like to own four hotels. The managing director of the Nokorthom Agriculture Development Company told us about her clientele of over one hundred wholesalers around the country. Next to her sat a professional recruiter for Abbey College in London. Dalin Noun had spent five years in California, five years in London, and five in Malaysia, recruiting top talent for the school. To my right was Sor Thida, the owner of Navyriya, a pharmacy and beauty store. She told us about her plan to construct a chain of her stores in Cambodia.

Promoting Entrepreneurship among Indian Women

In partnership with NFTE, I Create—a nonprofit in India that provides a practical grassroots entrepreneurship program for women and rural and urban youth—is working with over eighty nongovernmental organizations throughout India. The country is a growing economic power with the largest number of billionaires in the world outside the United States, yet it also has the largest number of poor in the world. Over ten million youth enter the Indian job market each year. In order to employ them, India will have to more than double its job creation rate. I Create offers a practical solution to this problem—teach Indian youth to start their own businesses. The nonprofit currently runs entrepreneurship education programs in fifteen regions of India and is expanding rapidly.

I Create also focuses on widows, abandoned women, and tribeswomen in impoverished rural areas. So far, I Create has assisted more than fourteen hundred women entrepreneurs. These women have become amazing role models for other destitute and disadvantaged women.

The *New York Times* wrote about one I Create entrepreneur named Sudha. She was a young lower-middle-class woman who was frequently beaten brutally by her in-laws for not bringing a dowry. Sudha was on the verge of committing suicide when she attended I Create's women's entrepreneurship training program. She not only became a successful entrepreneur, but she developed such self-confidence that she is now speaking to women's groups about entrepreneurship.

Dr. A. P. J. Abdul Kalam, former president of India, has lauded I Create's program publicly, telling the story of Abdus Samad, a very poor young man from a village in India, who, after I Create training, submitted his business plan to the local bank. He obtained a twenty-thousand-dollar loan and started a seed farm business six years ago. At present, his business volume is $10 million, and two hundred families directly or indirectly earn their livelihoods from his enterprise.

"Entrepreneurship incubation institutions (such as I Create) need to be developed all over India and the developing world," Dr. Kalam said.

The Entrepreneurship Revolution—Empowering Women

The interest and increase in entrepreneurship among women in recent years is very encouraging. In 2007 there were 7.8 million women-owned businesses in the United States, generating $1.2 trillion in revenues, up from 5.4 million such businesses in 1997. Fast forward to 2013, and the number of $10-million-plus women-owned firms increased by 57 percent that year, according to a report commissioned by American Express OPEN entitled *Growing under the Radar: An Exploration of the Achievement of Million-Dollar Women-Owned Firms.* This growth rate was nearly 50 percent more than the rate of growth for $10-million-plus firms overall, according to the January 2014 *Forbes* article "11 Reasons 2014 Will Be a Breakout Year for Female Entrepreneurs," by Geri Stengel.

In 2012, 20 percent of angels invested in women-led businesses—a percentage that had grown more than 40 percent from the previous year, according to the Center for Venture Research. Stengel also uncovered new emerging support from venture capitalists for female entrepreneurs. The percentage of venture capital deals going to women-led businesses was 13 percent in the first half of 2013—nearly a 20 percent jump over 2012, according to Pitchbook, a venture capital research firm.

Women may really have the right stuff when it comes to entrepreneurship. Zenger/Folkman, a company that specializes in leadership development, conducted research that founders Jack Zenger and Joseph Folkman have said indicates that women make better business leaders than men. "Two of the traits where women outscored men to the highest degree—taking initiative and driving for results—have long been thought of as particularly male strengths," Zenger and Folkman told *Forbes.* In addition, they said, women "build better teams; they're more liked and respected as managers; they tend to be able to combine intuitive and logical thinking more seamlessly; they're more aware of the implications of their own and others' actions; and they think more accurately about the resources needed to accomplish a given outcome."

According to the Small Business Administration Office of Advocacy, venture capital firms that invest in women-led businesses performed better than all men-led businesses. Moreover, Kauffman Foundation research has found that women-led private technology companies are more capital efficient, achieving 35 percent higher return on investment, and, when venture-backed, bringing in 12 percent higher revenue than male-owned tech companies.

Women are also increasingly providing capital for other female entrepreneurs. Although the current percentage of female angel investors is still small, it jumped 50 percent from 2011 to 2012 to 22 percent, according to the Center for Venture Research. "The women angel-networks themselves are getting the word out about the importance of women participating in the investment process and are doing a great job at welcoming new women into the investing community," Susan Duffy, executive director of the Center for Women's Leadership at Babson College, told Stengel in *Forbes*.

The number of women-led angel funds, such as Belle Capital, Golden Seeds, and Texas Women's Fund, has increased. Women are training other women to invest in female-led businesses through organizations such as 37 Angels and Pipeline Fellowship.

Female Crowdfunding

Considering that women control more than half the investment wealth in the United States, according to *Women and Money:*

Matters of Trust, this is good news for American female entrepreneurs. Women have also taken to crowdfunding in droves to fund their enterprises. Indiegogo is a popular crowdfunding platform. Of its successful campaigns, 42 percent were run by women. If women have better access to the capital they need, they'll create more jobs and help economies globally recover faster from the Great Recession, according to "Women Entrepreneurs as Economic Drivers," a report from the Kauffman Foundation.

Empower the World's "Willing Pioneers"

While the United States and other mature economies have been understandably focused on the hardships brought on by the Great Recession, women and more people in general around the globe are attaining a level of prosperity and economic security they had never known before in their history—often directly or indirectly because of entrepreneurship.

I've personally witnessed so many young people who have gone through NFTE's training and educational programs overcome cultural obstacles—from inner-city Philadelphia to a barrio in Colombia or a farm in rural Ireland. Many NFTE students arrive in our classrooms precisely because society has already judged them incapable in some way. Yet, consistently, when they are exposed to the possibilities of entrepreneurship, when they are taught that they have unique knowledge of their market—*because* of who they are, not in spite of who they are—they become fired up. They become what I call "willing pioneers," eager to exercise what Peter Klein calls "entrepreneurial judgment."

Entrepreneurship is creative, and entrepreneurs are brave. They are already living with one foot in the future as they strive to offer the world something no one else has. When I started

NFTE, I was especially indebted to Joe Mancuso and his Center for Entrepreneurial Management for their support and encouragement. Joe had a way of making entrepreneurship sound heroic for my kids in a way that other career and vocational classes simply could not match. Wealth, he would say,

> is created only by doers in the arena who are marred with dirt, dust, blood, and sweat. These are producers who strike out on their own, who know high highs and low lows, great devotions, and who overextend themselves for worthwhile causes. Without exception, they fail more than they succeed and appreciate this reality even before venturing out on their own. But when these producers of wealth fail, they at least fail with style and grace, and their gut soon recognizes that failure is only a resting place, not a place in which to spend a lifetime.

To anyone who has known little but failure and obstacles in their personal lives—whether due to gender, class, race, sexual orientation, or any other circumstance—this message is liberating and empowering.

CHAPTER 4

Should Governments Help Promote Entrepreneurship?

I N THE PREVIOUS chapter, Austrian School economist Peter Klein shared his views on whether governments should help promote entrepreneurship. In his opinion, a government should provide secure property rights, the rule of law, and sound money, but after that, "The best thing government can do for entrepreneurs is get out of their way."

I fundamentally agree with Klein, and I also think this viewpoint deserves deeper explanation and exploration.

THAT GOVERNMENT IS BEST WHICH GOVERNS LEAST

First, I should admit my biases. I grew up in a community that supported fervently the concept that, as Thomas Jefferson is believed to have said, "Government is best which governs least." My parents were big fans of Jefferson and Henry David Thoreau. Growing up, my intellectual heroes were defenders of individual liberties who were deeply skeptical of the power of government to do good in an impartial way. I think I was born skeptical of power. I believe that power corrupts and absolute power corrupts absolutely. I favor a constitutional government in which the rights and freedoms of every individual are guaranteed, and the state has no say in one's personal choices, as long as one does no damage to others.

In a free enterprise economic system, government is always a distorting force, blocking the signals that private buyers and sellers are trying to send. Tariffs and trade policy become instruments for favoring privileged interests or protecting them from domestic and foreign competition. Tax policy becomes a vehicle for a thousand pet causes and social engineering schemes, paid for by those who lack the political clout or financial expertise to shield their money. Regulations are written to favor those with the best access to the rule writers, imposing a dull uniformity on the business world when a thousand flowers should be encouraged to bloom.

There are legitimate public goods that only government can supply—as a public school teacher for many years, I would be the first to admit that—but the tendency is always for those with political power to overstep their bounds.

Education policy, I saw firsthand, morphs into a protection scheme for entrenched teachers' unions and education professionals, at the expense of students, parents, and private competitors such as charter schools that want to challenge the status quo. I'd like to see school vouchers introduced on a broad scale so that free-market competition can improve education in the United States. Instead of schools choosing students, as they do now for the 90 percent of students who go to public schools, students and their parents would choose the school which best fits the child's needs.

To my mind, government oppression is the worst kind of oppression. The scope of the lives lost and livelihoods ruined increases exponentially whenever the power of the state is abused as we've seen throughout history. It's hard to believe, but far more people were killed in the twentieth century by their own governments than died in World Wars I and II.

In addition, my work in our nation's inner cities and prison system has only deepened my long-held opposition to America's draconian drug laws, which have doomed so many nonviolent offenders to long prison sentences and ruined lives—with no social benefit.

I also think government has no business regulating anyone's private life. The late, great libertarian editor, critic, and gay activist Roy A. Childs Jr. was one of the true friends and political inspirations in my life. I thought of him when the Supreme Court finally struck down the anti–gay marriage Defense of Marriage Act in 2013 and wish he had lived to see it.

Even as a confirmed libertarian, however, I would love to see governments worldwide mandate the teaching of entrepreneurial principles in every school. Let's teach all children how capitalism works and how they can participate in this great economic system. Let's teach them the fundamentals of starting and operating a small business. They will learn how to recognize opportunities, identify markets, and respond to the information that prices carry. Let's show them the rewards—monetary and psychic—of successful entrepreneurship, and then let government get out of the way.

Entrepreneurs Check Political Power

Entrepreneurs are the ultimate freedom fighters. There is no greater challenge to unchecked political power than a private individual willing to spread a disruptive idea among his fellow citizens by becoming an entrepreneur. This challenge could be as small as a biofuel company that dares to offer an alternative to big oil or as big as the social networks Facebook and Twitter—both started by young entrepreneurs—that enabled average citizens to organize and mobilize against tyrannical governments on the streets of Cairo and Tehran.

Historically, entrepreneurs have been chief targets of governments trying to kill economic freedom. Entrepreneurs were slaughtered by the Nazis, Stalin, Mao, and the Khmer Rouge because they represent freedom and threaten socialism.

Economist and social philosopher Ludwig von Mises is another of my heroes, as well as the intellectual godfather of the modern libertarian movement. His 1922 book *Socialism* still stands as the most thorough and devastating demolition of socialism ever written. Mises proved that the only viable economic policy for the human race was free markets and unhampered exercise of the right of private property, with government strictly limited to the defense of people and property within its territory.

In *Socialism*, Mises demonstrated three critical points:

1. Expansion of free markets, division of labor, and private capital investment provide the only possible path to the prosperity and flourishing of the human race.
2. Socialism is disastrous for a modern economy because the absence of private ownership of land and capital goods prevents rational pricing, which (as Friedrich Hayek later proved) is how entrepreneurs and consumers communicate.
3. Government intervention, in addition to hampering and crippling free markets, is counterproductive and cumulative, leading inevitably to socialism and, ultimately, totalitarianism.

Mises proved that the more the state limited economic incentives to individuals and the more the entrepreneurial urge was stifled, the greater the harm to low-income people and the general population. As an Austrian citizen who had fled the Nazis, he argued strongly against centralized planning, which is characteristic of all three types of socialism we have observed in modern history—Nazism, fascism, and communism. Every time, central planning has destroyed entrepreneurship, ruined economies, and resulted in mass murder and the rise of totalitarian states.

This fatal conceit—that government bureaucrats in an office can determine how goods and services should be priced and allocated—violates a basic human concept: that every individual can choose best how to satisfy his or her wants and needs. That was Hayek's brilliant insight. These individual voluntary decisions collectively drive the prices of goods and services. Without this economic base of subjective value, a government will become totalitarian. At one time or another, over a billion people in about three dozen countries have lived under a political system which, at its heart, failed to recognize that value is subjective and cannot be effectively dictated by government.

This concept of subjective value is often misunderstood. Here is how I teach it to my junior- and high-school-level students. I hold up a picture of something of value—like a house—and ask each student to write down its worth. Typically, students list a wide range of estimates. This shows them that value is subjective, and that everyone has the right to an opinion. Subjective value may be a challenging concept to teach to young people, but is perhaps the most important because of its implications for human freedom.

How Government Debt Threatens Entrepreneurship

Currently, the biggest threat facing entrepreneurs in the U.S. and European economies is government spending. Sooner or later, government debt has to be repaid out of tax receipts. In the United States, the current revenue base is not strong enough to sustain a viable repayment program to service the debt. Instead, the Federal Reserve creates money—billions of dollars a month—to meet debt repayment demands. As new money floods the market, its value declines. Eventually, any country flooding its economy with excess money will experience inflation that will destroy the savings and pensions of its citizens. Similar conditions led to the downfall of the Weimar Republic. Rampant inflation in Germany during the 1920s was a significant contributing factor to the rise of the ultimate socialist organization: the Nazi Party.

Mises witnessed firsthand rampant government spending, overwhelming debt, and inflation in both Germany and Austria. The results of similar economic policies today are threatening major urban centers around our country. The July 2013 bankruptcy filing by the city of Detroit, Michigan, for example, is a harbinger of serious problems for the $2.9 trillion municipal bond market in the United States.

With cities like Detroit ($18.5 billion in debt), Philadelphia ($8 billion in debt), and Sacramento ($1.9 billion in debt) why are Mises disciple's voices silenced at major economic councils in Washington and throughout the country?

Robert Reich, former Clinton administration secretary of labor, singles out the huge economic and political discrepancies between the Tea Party and the Occupy movements sparked by the Wall Street government bailouts. In a series of articles in the *Huffington Post*, Reich cites the high correlation "between inequality and political divisiveness." He correctly points out that America hasn't been so divided regarding income, wealth, and power since the 1920s. What Reich fails to address are that similar conditions fed extremist movements, such as the Nazis and Communists, which later imploded due to government debt and unchecked printing of money.

Mises witnessed firsthand rampant government spending, overwhelming debt, and inflation in both Germany and Austria. The results of similar economic policies are threatening major urban centers around our country.

Followers of Mises today see government intervention in our nation's economy as seriously undermining economic productivity and self-starting growth. According to Peter Klein, a disciple of Mises, "People are increasingly disenchanted with mainstream Keynesian views of the economy. Keynesians were blindsided by the housing bubble and the financial crisis. Their response was to pump the economy with cheap credit and huge government spending which has only prolonged the agony. The Austrians led by Mises offer a compelling alternative explanation in which booms and busts are caused by central-bank manipulation of interest rates in vain attempts to stimulate or stabilize the economy."

Klein adds that monetary central planning, combined with misguided housing regulation, led the economy to produce the wrong kinds of goods and services. Klein believes our best road back to economic recovery involves getting the government out of the way and letting entrepreneurs fix the mistakes.

Anyone wishing to learn more about Mises should visit Hillsdale College in Michigan, which houses his personal library and works, or the Mises Institute located in Auburn, Alabama, which hosts the world's top philosophers, economists, students, and political scientists for annual conferences.

Political Freedom Is Necessary for Sustainable Entrepreneurship

I have strong doubts that totalitarian and authoritarian systems can compete in the long run in the competition to attract and foster entrepreneurial talent. Certainly, China's economic growth has been the marvel of the last three decades. In some ways, the Chinese understand the importance of entrepreneurship and free enterprise better than any society I have ever seen. But everything I believe about political theory and the disruptive power of entrepreneurship tells me that the Chinese system cannot survive in the long term in its present form.

When freedoms are uncertain, when the open exchange of information is curtailed, the economy eventually pays the price. For all their present success, there will be real problems for countries that try to promote economic freedom while keeping a lid on political freedoms.

When Governments Pick "Winners," Everybody Loses

Another danger for entrepreneurs is the idea that government can pick winners and losers in the marketplace. The cause may seem noble—a cleaner environment, safer city streets, reduced reliance on unreliable or hostile foreign suppliers—but for the free market, the cure is almost always worse than the disease. Yes, the government can conduct, or at least subsidize, basic research that clever entrepreneurs can turn into new products and new industries, but the minute the government steps in to tell the market which commercial ideas or which companies should succeed, the effects are disastrous. Mercifully, this fad finally seems to be dying down in the face of a string of well-publicized fiascos, including five alternative energy companies the Obama administration backed that went bankrupt and Germany's expensive and largely fruitless efforts to subsidize solar, wind, and biogas plants at a hefty price to taxpayers.

As Peter Klein noted earlier, "Government officials talk about giving us more and better entrepreneurship, but what they usually do is pick particular firms, industries, or technologies they like and give those firms subsidies and other benefits. The market should decide which firms, and which types of firms, succeed and fail."

Although governments around the world profess to love entrepreneurship in the abstract, budding business owners rarely find a seat at the table when the big decisions are made on taxes, regulations, and spending. If the Entrepreneurship Revolution is to succeed, this must change.

Government Policies That Hurt the Poor

The poor are especially hurt when the government interferes with free markets. The poor are hurt by minimum wage laws that choke off entry-level jobs and stifle new business creation, by welfare systems designed to perpetuate poverty, and by the unequal application of laws, which always and everywhere favor the more well-to-do. Government antipoverty programs isolate the poor from the rest of society and are structured to give too many a disincentive to ever earn enough money to get off the public dole.

In contrast—as I have seen over and over during thirty-plus years of working with at-risk youth—when poor children are exposed to entrepreneurship education and the principles of capitalism, they become empowered. They create their own pathways out of poverty and into education, jobs, and prosperity.

CAN GOVERNMENTS HELP ENTREPRENEURS AT ALL?

So can governments play any useful role in the Entrepreneurship Revolution? Just as we have seen with entrepreneurship education, the knowledge base of what works and doesn't work for governments seeking to promote entrepreneurial ecosystems and mind-sets has exploded in recent decades. There is nothing new, of course, about governments trying to boost favored business interests or protect "infant" industries; much of the great work of the early economists of the Industrial Revolution focused on the effects—good and bad—of mercantilism. But the explosion in entrepreneurship studies on campus, in the media, and in the business world has brought a new sophistication to understanding what makes entrepreneurs tick and how best to encourage them.

CAN THE STATE TIP THE BALANCE TO HELP ENTREPRENEURS?

Surveying the reams of data produced by the Global Entrepreneurship Monitor (GEM) project over the years, Simon Johnson, the former chief economist for the International Monetary Fund who now teaches at MIT, found that drawing straight-line conclusions is a difficult business. Entrepreneurship, he found, can be a ticket out of poverty in a struggling developing country, a new career option for a displaced worker in a mature economy, or an indulgent side project for the well-off in countries with mature, prosperous economies. Devising one program that gives incentives to all three types of entrepreneurs is next to impossible. In addition, some of the worst-run states in the world have some of the highest levels of entrepreneurial activity.

Still, "the negative effects of macroeconomic policy can crush new business creation, even in places with plenty of human capital and good perceived opportunities," Johnson wrote on the Economix blog for the *New York Times*, citing lower levels of enthusiasm for entrepreneurship in the troubled economies of southern Europe (Greece, Italy, Portugal) compared to their more prosperous northern neighbors with governments that had taken on less debt.

Building Entrepreneurial Economies

In 2004 economist and entrepreneur Carl Schramm, then president and CEO of the Ewing Marion Kauffman Foundation, published a short essay in *Foreign Affairs* titled "Building Entrepreneurial Economies" that would become one of the respected foreign policy journal's most frequently requested reprints. Schramm wrote that many nations had been backsliding from what had grandly been called the "Washington consensus," the market-oriented, free enterprise model that had triumphed in the long Cold War duel with the Marxist-Leninist command economy model of the Soviet Union. In particular, Schramm noted, many governments in Eastern Europe, Central and Latin America, and elsewhere were failing to reproduce one "vital element" of the American model: "support for entrepreneurship."

Classical economics and development policy tended to focus on established firms and underestimate the contributions from new and emerging players in the market. "Nations are urged to create good banking systems, reasonable interest and exchange rates, and stable tax structures," Schramm pointed out, while entrepreneurship, by contrast, "is considered only as an afterthought and in piecemeal fashion."

Policy fads, Schramm argued, are no substitute for a systematic, coordinated approach to entrepreneurship promotion. Creating a new class of venture capital firms "will do no good without ventures to support." Microenterprises are good as far as they go, but "these ventures tend to involve cottage industries that add little to the economy in terms of productivity and growth." Chasing outsourced work as a substitute for domestic entrepreneurship is also not a long-term strategy, because such work "has a disturbing tendency to migrate to still lower-cost locales."

"Real opportunities arise only when a nation is the initiator: a breeder of new firms, based on new ideas that add value," Schramm declared.

A New Consensus: Steps Governments Can Take to Promote Entrepreneurship

Since the publication of Schramm's seminal article, a new consensus has been building regarding policy areas that must work in concert for entrepreneurial ecosystems to take root. Government, business start-ups, mature businesses (which both compete and cooperate with their younger rivals), and the education system must all pull in the same direction, for starters.

The new consensus includes seven widely accepted steps that governments at all levels must adopt to promote a healthy culture of entrepreneurship:

1. **Provide a fair legal system** that includes a strong code of property rights and contract law, makes it easy to register and incorporate a business, and—just as important—has an orderly system of bankruptcy that reassures

lenders and enables a failed entrepreneur to get back on his or her feet.

2. **Shorten the time horizon and reduce red tape.** The longer it takes to incorporate a business and the more offices that must be visited and papers that must be stamped, the more likely it is that entrepreneurs will shun legitimate channels in favor of the underground black market. According to World Bank studies, the time it takes for a small- to mid-sized business to incorporate and formally operate around the world ranges from on average eleven days in OECD countries to over thirty-six days in both East Asia and Latin America. New Zealand wins, with just an average of a half-day and one official procedure to get a business registered, while in Venezuela it takes 114 days and involves seventeen different actions—seventeen different opportunities for delay and corruption. The United States ranked twentieth, with a five-day average to get registered and six procedures to be completed.

3. **Encourage a diverse and flexible funding universe.** Silicon Valley's venture capital infrastructure is the envy of the world, but entrepreneurship experts say it's more important to have multiple money streams watering the ground rather than one giant pipeline. As Schramm noted, venture capital firms typically don't even enter the picture for the crucial first three years of a start-up's life. An entrepreneur is always going to draw on personal savings, credit cards, and friends and family, but government can help by establishing funding sources—such as pension funds that invest a portion of their money in the entrepreneurial sector.

4. **Promote competition and diversity.** Long seen as competing interests, mature companies and start-ups actually often have more complicated symbiotic relationships. Bill Gates and Paul Allen are legendary entrepreneurs, but Microsoft might never have taken off if IBM hadn't licensed the fledgling company's operating system for Big Blue's PCs. Policies that promote competition and diversity among large, mature firms—including privatization of government monopolies, strong intellectual property and antitrust laws, and refraining from government policies favoring one company or sector over another—are now seen as a boost to the start-up sector as well.

5. **Destigmatize business failure.** Governments can help encourage entrepreneurs and their investors to see failure in a positive light, as part of the process, rather than as a stigma. The message should be that if your business doesn't work out, you have still developed important skills and learned useful business lessons.

6. **Invest in education.** The one public good where the investment dollar gets the biggest bang for the buck, development experts agree, is education at all levels. America's universities not only represent one of the country's greatest competitive strengths in the global marketplace and the hunt for talent, but they have become significant generators of new businesses themselves, with more than a third now housing or partnering with start-up and small-business incubator programs.

7. **Open borders.** An open border policy plays a key role in entrepreneurship promotion, because immigrants

consistently create an outsized percentage of the new business start-ups, year after year. Immigrants or their offspring created 40 percent of the U.S. companies listed on the Fortune 500, and immigrants accounted for nearly a third of all new businesses in the United States in 2011, more than twice the percentage created by the overall population.

Immigrants Key to Dynamic Economies

As one who believes passionately in the power of free markets, I believe that the welcome mat the United States offers to ambitious, hard-working immigrants has long been one of our greatest strengths. Whether it is Polish-born Maxwell Kohl of Kohl's Corporation, French-born Iranian eBay founder Pierre Omidyar, or Google's Russian-born Sergey Brin, a large portion of America's successful entrepreneurs have been immigrants. This phenomenon of cross-border entrepreneurial formation and success has begun to attract the attention of academics, policymakers, and economists.

Robert W. Fairlie, an economics professor at the University of California at Santa Cruz, put together an eye-opening survey of the contributions that immigrant entrepreneurs have made both to the American economy and to its trade balance. The 2012 study "Open for Business: How Immigrants Are Driving Small Business Creation in the United States" was sponsored by the bipartisan Partnership for a New American Economy. Fairlie's findings make an overwhelming case for the importance of entrepreneurship in the economy, and the need to foster its growth, for both immigrants and nonimmigrants alike, in the decades to come.

Citing Census Bureau data, academic research, and a slew of case studies, "Open for Business" found that immigrants to the United States are increasingly key to the dynamism of the economy. Among the headline findings:

- The rate of immigrant business formation grew by 50 percent between 1996 and 2011, while "native-born" formations fell by 10 percent. Immigrants were responsible for 28 percent of all new businesses formed in 2011, up from 15 percent in 1996, yet in 2011, immigrants made up less than 13 percent of the U.S. population.
- Immigrant business accounted for over $775 billion in revenues, $125 billion in payroll, and $100 billion in income, employing a tenth of the U.S. workforce.
- Immigrant start-ups target the fastest-growing sectors of the economy, including health care, construction, retail, leisure, and hospitality services. The contribution of entrepreneurial immigrants is all but certain to grow faster than the national economy in the years to come.
- With their language skills and ties to their home country, immigrant-owned start-ups also export at higher levels, boosting the nation's trade balance. Immigrant-owned businesses of all sizes are 60 percent more likely to export than nonimmigrant-owned businesses and are two and a half times more likely to be "high-exporting firms"—making more than 20 percent of their sales outside the United States.

Fairlie concludes, "As policymakers consider measures to increase job growth, politicians may disagree on spending or cutting taxes, protecting or opening markets, or the value of various regulations. But one thing should be beyond argument:

Any serious plan on job growth must recognize and welcome immigrant entrepreneurs, who in the coming years will play an outsized role across the country and across industries in starting new businesses, creating new jobs, and driving economic growth."

Just as goods should be able to flow freely across borders, so should people, in my opinion. The 2012 GEM report devoted an entire chapter to the pros and cons of international people flows. In it, economic geographer Arne Vorderwuelbecke of Leibniz University in Hanover, Germany, noted, "International migration is a key contributor to globalization in cultures and in business. Today there are more than 210 million international migrants worldwide, and the long-term trend indicates a further increase within the next decades."

Student Loans Dampen Entrepreneurship

Immigrant and native-born American families struggle with how to send their kids to college. The average college graduate in 2014 faced a debt of $33,000 on graduation day. Over seven million people are in default on federal or private student loans, according to the federal Consumer Finance Protection Board (CFPB). Overall student debt now tops $1 trillion.

Government-backed and private loans are widely available, but the way they are structured puts too many of our kids deep in debt just as they are trying to start a career or found a business. This has a direct dampening effect on entrepreneurship.

The CFPB polled borrowers, lenders, and policymakers about the growing burden of traditional student debt. According to CFPB school loan ombudsman Rohit Chopra, school loan carrying costs "diminish entrepreneurship and small business growth." He added:

In submissions by coalitions of small businesses and start-ups, they cited a number of factors about the threats from student debt. For many young entrepreneurs, it's critical to invest capital to develop new ideas, market products, and hire employees. High student debt burdens require these individuals to take more cash out of their business so they can make monthly student loan payments. Others note that unmanageable student debt limited their ability to access small-business credit; some report being denied a small-business loan because of student loan debt.

The *Wall Street Journal* chronicled one case in point. Jackson Solway, a 2009 graduate from Colorado College with a degree in political science, had an idea for an online business to hook up companies with teams of freelancers to cut down on direct personnel costs. But Solway abandoned his idea after just a year because he needed a regular paycheck to meet his four-hundred-dollar-a-month student loan payments. "I love the start-up world. I would be a serial entrepreneur if it weren't for my student loans," Solway told the *Journal*.

Similarly, Dave Girouard, cofounder of the innovative crowdfunding firm Upstart, told the *New Yorker*, "I saw a repeating pattern, where you had people just out of school who had something interesting and compelling that they wanted to do, but who were instead going to accept the job at Raytheon or whatever. They weren't excited about the new job, but pragmatically it was the right thing to do."

A Market-Oriented Solution: Human Capital Contracts

As usual, Milton Friedman got there first.

Back in 1955 the Nobel Prize–winning economist published

a paper that proposed a market-oriented solution to the problem we face today: Young people coming out of high school are
asked to make one of the biggest long-term investments of their
lives—a college education—at a time when very few have built
up any significant capital.

The federal government and states like Rhode Island are
experimenting with new "income-based" repayment plans that
enable a student borrower to pay back loans based on his or her
income. Friedman developed this concept a half-century ago,
and today the Internet may turn it into a global game-changer.

Friedman's insight was that an investor could make an "equity-
like" investment in financing a young person's college tuition in
exactly the same way as any other investment is structured. He
noted back in the 1950s that there was a significant "underinvest-
ment" in human capital in the student loan market. He argued
that those with capital could "invest" in young people trying to
finance their education in exchange for a mutually agreed-upon
and adjustable chunk of that student's future earnings.

In his paper, Friedman anticipated some of the logistical and
moral problems that private human capital contracts might
encounter: What is the "collateral" the borrower puts up for the
investment? How does one enforce the contract if the borrower
refuses to pay after finding work? What kind of oversight would
be needed to ensure that the terms of the contracts did not
amount to backdoor loans at usurious rates? Would education
venture capital dollars flow to favored schools or fields, institutions, and students? Does the human capital contract model
simply revive the old notion of indentured servitude in fancy
free-market clothing?

In the 1970s Yale University attempted to replace traditional
student loans with human capital contracts under its "Tuition
Postponement Option," designed by Friedman and economist

James Tobin. It was swamped, however, by government intervention and the introduction of the current federally guaranteed student loan program.

Human Capital Contracts Thrive Online

It took the advent of the Internet to exploit the full power of Friedman's insight. Companies like Upstart, Pave.com, Career-Concept, and Lumni are running with the idea of human capital contracts (HCCs) online.

To the notion that these contracts (one company prefers the term "social financial agreements") are a modern form of indentured servitude, the response from these companies is basically, "Get over it." They note that the idea of wealthy backers staking a promising newcomer on the cusp of his career is nothing new. Promising poker players, prizefighters, artists, and authors have long gotten through their struggling early years on the strength of advances from financial angels, paying their investors back when—and if—they hit it big.

Human capital contracts are like venture capital deals for our young, betting not on an idea but on the potential of the student to turn an education into a life that proves personally rewarding and profitable to society as a whole. Done correctly, they also have built-in safeguards and flexibility designed to help the young student and young entrepreneur at a time in life when safeguards and flexibility are vitally needed.

Unlike fixed-amount, fixed-structure student loan repayment schedules, HCCs can be adjusted so that the borrower only pays when he or she starts earning a real income from a real job.

Most of these contracts also have a fixed upper bound—for example, 7 percent of one's income. If a human capital contract lender happens to back a Mark Zuckerberg or Sergey Brin, the lender doesn't get to claim an unreasonable slice of his borrower's later fortune.

Human capital contracts have the potential to increase the amount of funding available for students and reduce the cost of education funding. Even better, human capital contracts require little government intervention and will increase the efficiency of the education market. In the words of Friedman, they can increase equality of opportunity and address income inequalities without "impeding competition, destroying incentive, and dealing with symptoms, as would result from outright redistribution of income, but by strengthening competition, making incentives effective, and eliminating the causes of inequality."

Financial Backers Become Mentors

These new companies providing social financial agreements, such as Pave.com, tout their role not just as financial backers but as mentors. They actively coach the students they've invested in and help them network in their chosen fields.

Lumni founders Felipe Vergara and Miguel Palacios—who have targeted low-income students in their native Colombia as well as in Chile, Mexico, and the United States—have raised over $15 million from one hundred investors, signing human capital contracts to finance the education of nearly two thousand students.

Founders of Lumni told the *New York Times* the story of one Lumni beneficiary, Colombian nursing student Jairo Sneider. Sneider grew up in a poor, single-parent household in Colombia and lacked collateral or a cosigner for the estimated eighty-five hundred dollars he needed to complete his studies.

Under the Lumni contract, Sneider's tuition and college costs were paid in full in exchange for 14 percent of his salary for ten years after he graduated. There was no set monthly payment, and the obligation to pay dissolved with the end of the contract, regardless of how much Jairo was able to pay up until then. The Lumni arrangement offers Jairo far more flexibility than a traditional loan. If he wants to go back to school for a higher degree, or if he leaves nursing for another field, his repayments will drop as his income does.

If Jairo stays in nursing and earns the expected salary over the next decade, he will pay the equivalent of a student loan with an interest rate of 17 percent—the average student-loan rate in his country—without the pressure of meeting monthly payments and without financial constraints keeping him from pursuing higher education or starting a business.

Everyone Has "Unique Knowledge"

"The most important asset in the world is people," Vergara told the *Times*, "but modern society hasn't organized itself in a way to invest in most people. I like to think of Lumni as a springboard that allows people to pursue their dreams. It offers a way out of a situation where the ceiling is very close to your head."

On a deeper level, human capital contracts have the potential to free our young people from the more subtle servitude of lives spent at jobs they don't love, lives spent failing to develop their own unique knowledge. Every human being, Friedrich Hayek wrote in his famous article "The Use of Knowledge in Society," has a comparative advantage, some unique contribution to make. Let's make sure our young graduates are free to explore their own comparative advantages without feeling like they have to take the first job that comes along in order to pay off tuition debt.

The Nolan Chart

I've seen the light go on in my own students the first time they've heard this concept—that they, too, have "unique knowledge" that could be developed into a profitable business. In fact, many young people I meet these days hold economic views that are pro-market and entrepreneurial. They also believe in social tolerance and wonder where that places them politically. Are they Republicans? Democrats?

There is a wonderful tool called the Nolan Chart we could all use to more accurately represent our political positions and ease the current divisiveness that plagues our nation. Instead of the traditional "left-right" line, which measures politics along a one-dimensional line, the Nolan Chart represents a much richer variety of political viewpoints.

I was there the day this breakthrough was first envisioned by legendary '60s youth leader Carl Oglesby. It was October 10, 1965, at the Unitarian Church in Ann Arbor, Michigan. Carl was the elected leader of the Students for a Democratic Society (SDS). I was his teenage expert in marketing the anti-Vietnam War movement to my peers.

Carl was preparing to give a talk at what was going to be a massive anti-war demonstration in Washington, D.C., on November 27—although we didn't know at the time that the turnout would be so huge. He had written his soon-to-be-historic speech, "Let Us Shape the Future," and was practicing it in the church rec room. I was thirteen, and was president of the Unitarian Church youth groups in both Ann Arbor and Flint. Needless to say, I worshipped Carl.

After the service, we all gathered for coffee, eager to hear Carl's speech. As we listened, we noticed that Carl used the word

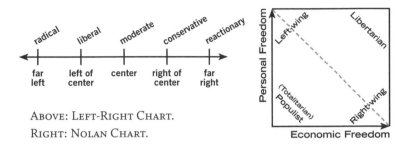

ABOVE: LEFT-RIGHT CHART.
RIGHT: NOLAN CHART.

"coordinates" to describe issues on which he believed the left and the right shared common ground. This led us into a discussion of the limitations of the Left/Right Line Chart, which was often used at the time to illustrate a person's political views.

The Left/Right Chart plotted a person's political leanings on a line from left (liberal) to right (conservative). The assumption was that people on the right were more focused on economic freedom (and less concerned with personal freedom) and those on the left were more concerned with personal freedom (and less concerned with economic freedom). Carl was trying to explain in his speech that plotting our political ideologies in this limited way had created a false left/right dichotomy that made Democrat and Republican viewpoints seem hopelessly at odds. Sound familiar?

My father understood what Carl was getting at but felt he needed a better way to explain it. Knowing my love for math, he asked me to diagram Carl's concept on the chalkboard in the coffee room.

Eager to show off, I grabbed a piece of chalk and drew an X and a Y axis. I labeled the horizontal axis "economic freedom" and the vertical axis "personal freedom." My drawing was the precursor to David Nolan's groundbreaking diagram based on Carl's insight, which became known as the Nolan Chart.

David Nolan came up with the word "Libertarian" to describe people whose political views fell into the chart's upper-right quadrant. Nolan published his initial version of the chart in his article "Classifying and Analyzing Politico-Economic Systems" in the January 1971 issue of the *Individualist*, the monthly magazine of the Society for Individual Liberty (SIL). The Nolan Chart became the defining document of the Libertarian party, which Nolan founded in December 1971, using ideas developed by Carl Oglesby, Murray Rothbard, Ayn Rand, and F. A. Hayek.

The Nolan Chart opens up the political landscape, prompting people to rethink their assumptions. Using the old left/right line chart, for example, it is hard to say whether Ron Paul or Ted Cruz is more "conservative," but on the Nolan Chart, both their views can be plotted clearly.

In my opinion, the Nolan Chart is one of the most important political breakthroughs of all time. It allows people to articulate and represent their political views clearly and helps us all find common ground. People with differing views regarding how the law should govern an individual's actions, for example, might realize that they hold common economic views, for example. The Nolan Chart makes it easier to express political concepts such as classical liberalism—which emphasizes securing the freedom of the individual by limiting the power of government, or voluntary society—in which all services are provided through voluntary means, such as private or cooperative ownership, rather than state ownership.

Carl Oglesby was eventually fired as head of the SDS, as the movement became radicalized and co-opted by the Weather Underground. His speech in front of over thirty-five thousand people on the Washington Mall remains one of the most significant of the 1960s, however. It galvanized young leaders to join the anti-war movement and emphasized the potential of free markets and entrepreneurship. I trace my vision for founding NFTE back to that day and that powerful speech by my first mentor. I believed then, and I do now, that we can shape the futures of thousands of low-income, at-risk youth through entrepreneurship education and by encouraging economic and personal freedom.

CHAPTER 5

A Teaching Revolution

I don't care who writes a nation's laws—or crafts its advanced treatises—if I can write its economics textbooks.

—Nobel Prize–winning economist Robert Samuelson

EVEN IF WE ARE able to free our college graduates from heavy educational debt, they won't be equipped to explore their own potential as entrepreneurs if they are not business literate and have not cultivated entrepreneurial mind-sets. Not only do we need an Entrepreneurship Revolution, we need a Teaching Revolution to clear away the current barriers against teaching entrepreneurship and financial literacy in our children's classrooms—before they get to college!

Unfortunately, despite an early burst of enthusiasm for entrepreneurship education during the 1980s when the new U.S. Department of Education mandated that all career and technical programs include a section on entrepreneurship, progress toward bringing entrepreneurship education to our schoolchildren has been frustratingly slow, due to a variety of barriers.

Entrepreneurship education curricula and credentials for entrepreneurship instructors are still developing, for starters. When I started NFTE I had to write my own textbook, for example. There were no entrepreneurship education textbooks for high-school, junior-high, or grade-school students. In 2002 our high-school textbook, *How to Start and Operate a Small Business*, and its companion teacher resource guide, received the Association of Education Publishers (AEP) Golden Lamp Award for the best educational and teacher materials in America. The 2010 edition won a Golden Lamp Award for the best math curriculum.

There are even more significant and fundamental barriers to entrepreneurship education that need to be addressed, however, starting with our teachers.

An Antibusiness Attitude in Our Schools

Why would an entrepreneurship textbook receive an award for best math curriculum? Because entrepreneurship is a fantastic way to get kids excited about improving their math skills. Yet when I was a public school teacher I was repeatedly warned by other teachers and my supervisors not to talk about money in the classroom or use business-related examples to teach. To say that was frowned upon is putting it mildly. To be honest, I was drummed out of a series of schools for attempting to use real-world business examples to teach math until I finally found a principal who understood what I was trying to do.

This attitude has still not changed at most public schools— not only in my opinion, but also according to the Consortium of Entrepreneurial Education (CEE). In the mid-1980s, while I was still teaching high school, Cathy Ashmore founded the CEE, an invaluable resource for a novice teacher like me who was stumbling toward developing a method for instructing students about entrepreneurship. Over the years the CEE has become a home base for educators who embrace the idea of entrepreneurship education and wish to learn the best techniques for teaching kids from kindergarten through twelfth grade.

In 2012 Dr. Ashmore summed up her own frustrations about the state of entrepreneurship education in a *Time* article with the straightforward title: "Why We're So Bad at Teaching Entrepreneurship."

"Over the past 30 years," Dr. Ashmore noted:

> I've discovered many barriers preventing teachers from effectively teaching entrepreneurship. In fact, it became obvious that educators at the local and state levels were themselves among the major barriers to providing experiences in business creation. . . . In spite of very strong student interest in starting their own businesses as a career, state education program funding historically has not recognized entrepreneurship as a fundable high-school program. As a result, those teachers who chose to teach entrepreneurship often did so on their own initiative and outside of established curriculum. Even now, teacher training in most states barely addresses the teaching of entrepreneurship, if at all.

Ashmore identifies a series of barriers holding back effective entrepreneurship education in this country. These include lack of funding, resistance to changing the curricula to incorporate entrepreneurship training into the larger lesson plan, and the fact that many college business programs see entrepreneurship education as their exclusive territory, not to be shared with other disciplines or taught at other levels of schooling.

In addition, she noted, teachers rarely have the business background, real-world experience, or entrepreneurial mind-set to teach entrepreneurship effectively. As Ashmore explained, "Effective entrepreneurship training does impart specific knowledge and skills, but it must also convey a mind-set—one that embraces a certain amount of risk and is ready to learn and bounce back from repeated failures.

"Unfortunately," she continued, "most teachers have never been entrepreneurs, others are failed entrepreneurs who went to teaching as a more secure career, and some don't even know a business owner—not the ideal people to convey such a mind-set. And because of this cultural divide, they aren't likely to encourage students to become entrepreneurs."

A New Consensus: Practice Plus Theory

A new consensus is building that entrepreneurship teachers must not only understand business concepts, but also have an entrepreneurial mind-set if they are to be effective. Real-world business experience is useless in the classroom, on the other hand, if the teacher lacks the organizational and communication skills to pass on that experience.

A hybrid approach is what Candida Brush, Patti Greene, and Heidi Neck, researchers at Babson College's Arthur M. Blank Center for Entrepreneurship, recommend in their 2014 book *Teaching Entrepreneurship: A Practice-Based Approach*. They've developed a series of "modules" that would-be instructors can study, including creativity and idea generation, opportunity evaluation and business planning, social entrepreneurship, entrepreneurial financing and technology, family enterprises, "giving voice to values," and managing growing ventures.

"For decades we have debated whether entrepreneurship should be taught by entrepreneurs who have real-world experience, or whether it should be taught from the perspective of theory, like other disciplines," Dr. Brush wrote in *Forbes*:

On the one hand, there are entrepreneurs telling war stories about how they achieved success with their insights and attributes. On the other hand, a more scholarly approach focuses on activity that involves the discovery, evaluation, and exploitation of opportunities to introduce new goods and services, ways of organizing, markets, process, and raw materials through organizing efforts that previously had not existed.

We agree that in order to learn entrepreneurship, one must do entrepreneurship. But doing does not exclude theory. On the contrary, effective doing of entrepreneurship requires a set of practices and these practices are firmly grounded in theory.

The Challenge of Idea Replication

I agree with this hybrid approach. It's critical that we in entrepreneurship education develop this consensus as we seek to revolutionize the teaching of entrepreneurship and encourage schoolteachers to embrace it as a great way to motivate their students to improve math, reading, and writing skills.

Sometimes, though, the hardest thing to do with an idea is replicate it. One idea can revolutionize the world, creating shifts in understanding until thinking otherwise is inconceivable—but only if it can be replicated. Replication is the process of sharing information and ensuring the consistency of an idea through open practice.

The power of idea replication is immense. In this regard I think of Max Planck, the German physicist who actualized quantum physics because of his inability to solve a math problem. In 1900 he proposed the Planck postulate, which provided a constant between the intractable issue of energy and radiation frequency. The postulate started as an idea in Planck's head, was published for review, and then was discussed by the eminent physicists of his time, integrated into world conferences, and improved upon by other scientists. It eventually led to Planck receiving the Nobel Prize for physics in 1918.

Universities accepted Planck's idea, governments funded research that put his idea into practice, and entrepreneurs developed products based on derivatives of his insight and brought them to market. Because Planck's postulate was successfully replicated, this single idea became a sustainable basis for many products and innovations from which entire new industries were created, while our understanding of energy was forever changed.

Teacher Training Is Key to Replicating Entrepreneurship Education

What is the key to replicating an idea in youth work? I believe it is teacher training. I speak as someone whose first formal attempt to train entrepreneurship teachers was an unmitigated disaster.

When we began teacher training at NFTE I gave the first session in Boston for a group of high-school educators. Things did not go well. I talked nonstop for three days. People sat dumbfounded by my ignorance of how to teach adults.

In spite of poor reviews I was undaunted and repeated the same mistake later in the year with a larger audience at Babson College. Over one hundred teachers assembled by the college were deadened by my forty-hour nonstop lecture. Oddly, I failed to use the lively tactics and engaging exercises that made me a good classroom teacher when I went into teacher-training mode.

After those disastrous early sessions in Boston and at Babson College, my staff and other teachers helped me figure it out. At that time, NFTE's headquarters were on Twenty-Third Street and Seventh Avenue in New York City. My small staff (Chris Meenan, Jack Mariotti, Janet McKinstry, Mike Caslin, Scott Shickler, Juan Casimiro, and Kevin Greaney) and I would invite other teachers interested in entrepreneurial education to share ideas about lesson plans and classroom strategies during brainstorming sessions in the Hotel Chelsea.

We would cross the street, enter the Chelsea, and lug an overhead projector up the hotel's famous grand staircase to Room 100. Such legendary writers as Dylan Thomas, William S. Burroughs, and Arthur Miller had lived in this hotel, and we liked to think we were getting energy from their creative genius.

We had endless and fascinating discussions regarding how to engage low-income, at-risk youth in goal setting, opportunity recognition, business plan creation, and basic skills like math and reading. We boiled down the basic concepts we wanted every class to learn, like creating financial statements, calculating breakeven, and determining the economics of one unit.

"Experiential, experiential, experiential," we would remind ourselves, to reinforce the primary insight: Young people learn best by doing. Over time, we developed simple business games and activities. We outlined in detail the minute-by-minute activities of the class, planning precisely what each teacher would teach and need. We had learned how important visuals are in teaching, so we made a rule that every teacher should use an overhead projector to present the materials

By 1993 our teacher trainings were getting rave reviews, and we were training over four hundred teachers a year. Some living legends took our teacher training, including Marilyn Kourlisky, codirector of the Institute for the Study of Educational Entrepreneurship at UCLA and chief education adviser for the Kauffman Center. Football legend Charles Woodson attended, as did pop singer Chynna Phillips.

What We've Learned about Teaching Entrepreneurship

Pretty much every youth entrepreneurship program in the world aimed at high-school or junior-high kids has sent someone through our four-day certification program to be trained. Here are eleven things NFTE has learned about running effective teacher training in youth entrepreneurship:

1. *Find and recruit the best teachers in the world* by using an intense selection process. This is key: Get the best and the brightest on your team. Many of the top professionals in the world go into K–12 teaching. Some of them are gifted not only in small business but also in educating low-income youth. These are the hybrid teachers the Entrepreneurship Revolution needs—find and incentivize them.

2. *Separate your teaching community into two categories*; the Certified Entrepreneur Trainer (CET) teaches children, and the Certified Entrepreneurship Teacher Instructor (CETI) teaches teachers. There is definitely a different skill set for working directly with kids versus working with teachers.

3. *Find a balance between teaching entrepreneurship itself and teaching the strategies used to teach entrepreneurship.*

Initially NFTE tended to emphasize the entrepreneurship aspects of our program, as many teachers did not have a business background. But we've since struck more of a balance, because going over the pedagogy of entrepreneurial education is equally as important as making sure the teacher trainees understand business concepts.

4. *Integrate all possible learning strategies into the teacher training classroom.* Group work, Socratic discussion, PowerPoints, games, activities, videos, and lectures are all of great value. Give the teachers quiet time so that they can absorb what they are studying.

5. *Standardize the training.* Once you have multiple trainers and trainings, you must use the same materials and structure. Otherwise, it is very hard to do research and measure the effectiveness of your teacher training.

6. *Treat teacher trainees well.* Have name tags and a clean room with all their materials ready for them. Know their names before they come in, and greet them each by name. Provide refreshments and lunch. The better the teachers feel about your program, the more time they will spend implementing it and the more likely they are to recruit other teachers.

7. *Use a survey to get feedback from teachers* at the end of every training so that you can improve your teacher-training program.

8. *Stay in touch with your teachers and provide continual support.* Your program is just beginning when the teacher training is completed. At NFTE we provide one full-time program manager for every fifteen teachers. The program managers organize field trips, teach the finer points of our courses, and act as coaches and trainers.

9. *Require regular follow-up sessions for professional development.* Each of our program managers provides approximately sixteen additional hours of training for our teachers every term.

10. *Let the teachers experience working in groups and presenting their business plans.* The more the teachers are encouraged to create their own business plans and make their first sales, the more they will understand the motivational aspect of entrepreneurship education, and the better entrepreneurship teachers they will be.

11. *Always stick to the schedule.* So many criticisms of adult education result from disorganized events.

FIND TEACHERS WHO INSPIRE

It's been said that the mediocre teacher tells, the good teacher explains, the superior teacher demonstrates, the great teacher inspires.

It takes just one great teacher to make the difference in so many young lives. I first met Maria Jimenez at the 2013 NFTE New York metro area Young Entrepreneur Showcase, which highlighted the entrepreneurial ideas and projects of local middle-schoolers.

The students were enrolled in Exploring Careers, a new NFTE youth entrepreneurship program. Exploring Careers gives young people a chance to develop business ideas in a comprehensive way, guided by an NFTE teacher. For the students, the showcase was an opportunity to pitch their business ideas to the audience and a panel of judges as well as to compete in five categories: fashion and apparel, lifestyle and education, mobile apps and software, tech innovation, and audience choice. Maria had been working with the kids to ready their projects for the competition.

Maria graduated from Queens College in 1999 with a bachelor's degree in English and a double minor in secondary education and sociology. After she became a teacher, she pursued a master's degree in reading education and became certified as a reading specialist in grades K–12. Teaching entrepreneurship came later, but she quickly recognized that it has "a tremendous value to the population I teach."

Maria noted,

> In today's world, my students find themselves at a loss as to where to turn and what career goals to follow. In today's job market, there is tremendous pressure on them to choose the appropriate path that will lead them to financial success and independence. This course provides another alternative and possibility in their lives. Most of my students have never considered this option, but after they take my course, they realize that their lives are full of endless possibilities and choices. They learn the basics of running their own business, as well as the risks, rewards, values, and relationships involved in such an undertaking. They walk away understanding that entrepreneurship is a huge responsibility full of benefits as well as hardships. I have no doubt that some of them will in fact become successful entrepreneurs.

NYSE Teachers' Workshop

You'll also find extraordinary teachers interested in helping students understand our economy at the New York Stock Exchange's (NYSE) Teachers' Workshop. During four separate weeks over the summer, the NYSE invites thirty-five top business and economics teachers from across the country to New York City to spend five days learning about the financial markets and trading so that they can bring this knowledge back to their classrooms. The workshop uses materials developed by the NYSE to teach young people how financial markets work, giving them powerful insights into ownership and capitalism.

Every person in the world needs to learn how business owners tap into capital—how they use the savings of others to grow businesses and also help their investors' money grow. It's an eye-opening, life-changing experience. I have had the pleasure of being a guest speaker at the NYSE Teachers' Workshop for many years and always look forward to it. To speak to my community—business educators—is a special treat for me. I always share six things I think every young person needs to know about business:

1. **Find your comparative advantage.** Each young person has unique knowledge of his or her market (friends, family, neighborhood)—an idea for which Friedrich Hayek won the Nobel Prize. Helping children find their comparative advantage is, in my opinion, the most important goal of education. It can almost always be found by helping them examine what they love to do or their hobbies.

2. **Learn to listen.** If you teach children to listen, they will be able to sell their products more successfully and design effective marketing campaigns for their businesses. They will also become much more employable. Running their own small businesses helps children learn to listen, because they soon notice that if they don't, they don't make as many sales as the kids who do.

3. **Plan and project.** Entrepreneurs are time travelers. They must imagine the future in order to project what

people will need, then they must find the resources to create a product or service that meets that future need. By writing business plans for their own small businesses, children begin to understand this concept. They become comfortable with longer time horizons and delaying gratification. They grasp the relationship between risk and reward.

4. **Understand your economics of one unit.** Understanding how much one unit actually costs to produce and what the price must be in order for the entrepreneur to earn a profit is a powerful lesson for every child.

5. **Know how to communicate with customers and the media.** At NFTE each child writes down his or her story and develops it into a short, media-friendly press release. The kids discover that they each have unique and interesting stories that will attract customers to their businesses. The students develop self-awareness and the ability to communicate their stories and business vision to others. When they get positive responses, including investments of time, energy, advice, or money from others into their businesses, it changes forever their views of what they can accomplish.

6. **Use Teamwork.** The ability to work with people is crucial to achieving success with a business. Children become motivated by entrepreneurship to try harder to get along with others. They discover that to work successfully with others they must be polite, respectful, and noncoercive.

After the 2013 NYSE Teachers Workshop, I interviewed two teachers: Eugene Pope from Chicago, who was NFTE's Teacher of the Year a few years prior, and Christina Conley from Oklahoma

City, who has been teaching for nineteen years and works primarily with a Native American population struggling with poverty and unemployment.

Steve Mariotti: Why is financial literacy so important to young people today?

Eugene Pope: Typically, the students in my program are the forgotten students who have predetermined that they can't do math or can't read. While writing a business plan, their eyes open, seeing that they can calculate the return on investment (ROI) and many things mathematically, especially algebra, and they begin to flourish.

Christine Conway: I saw students struggling in math and other studies, and I wanted to help them to gain confidence in math, stay in school, and improve in their academics before going to high school.

SM: Why are some kids not able to learn math?

CC: Perhaps they are not able or willing. I think kids get to a certain point where they start to struggle, and when they get home, their parents don't have the knowledge or resources to help.

SM: Should financial literacy be required learning in school systems?

EP: Yes, it should be required if we're trying to remedy poverty. Financial literacy has a lot to do with personal finances. Many students are living in poverty because there is a lack of financial understanding in families and neighborhoods.

SM: What is or has been the highlight of the NYSE Teachers' Workshop?

EP: As a project-based teacher, action is key. Learning how the NYSE works helps create a lesson that works. For example, the wholesale experience is applicable—actual trading, bidding for supplies, selling, creating another event based on that experience, etc., gives a better understanding of the stock exchange.

SM: How will you incorporate the tools and knowledge you have learned from the NYSE Teachers' Workshop into your classroom?

EP: I will be able to take the tools and knowledge that I have learned back into the classroom to help students visualize that they are actually at the NYSE. By teaching students the real-world application of learning how to calculate the Dow and compare it to what's going on in their community and beyond that—it will help them "demystify" the stock market.

Start Up Math: A Pioneering Program

Earlier in this chapter I mentioned the connection between entrepreneurship education and math. One of the biggest problems of our time is that many low-income students are not learning basic math. According to Eric Hanushek and Paul Peterson, senior fellows at the Hoover Institution, less than 15 percent of minority youth in the United States are performing math at the proficient level or higher.

Without a strong basic foundation in math, being able to attend college or have a successful career in any industry is unlikely. A student who never grasps percentages, decimals, and fractions is at a disadvantage pursuing any career, including entrepreneurship. Ownership splits, markups, financial statement analysis, salary negotiations, and incentive-based job performance are all very challenging to understand without basic knowledge of these concepts. Much of the determination of who owns assets in America is based on the ability to leverage academic ability, especially around mathematics.

That's why NFTE's entrepreneurship education curriculum has more than two hundred basic math lessons. In addition, we've developed Start Up Math, a program that uses entrepreneurship lessons to identify skill gaps in basic mathematics concepts among struggling sixth- to eighth-graders.

Start Up Math reflects best practices in teaching and is aligned to twenty-two nongeometry Common Core seventh-grade mathematics standards, while exploring entrepreneurship concepts. This is a project-based entrepreneurship/mathematics hybrid class designed to appeal to students struggling to overcome poor mathematics skills, conquer math anxiety, and find relevancy to their lives in coursework.

The program is being pioneered in Washington, DC, where I hope it will become a revolutionary global springboard for this approach to project-based mathematics and entrepreneurship instruction. Some of the best math teachers in the nation's capital were selected for a five-day teacher training hosted at George Washington University by codirector Dr. George Solomon of the Center for Entrepreneurial Excellence (CFEE).

The training shows teachers how to use Bloom's taxonomy principles to teach math concepts, including percentages, decimals, fractions, proportional relationships, statistics, probability, number lines (including negative numbers), Venn diagrams, pie charts, measures of central tendencies (averages, means, medians, etc.), and basic equations. Additionally, Start Up Math includes a data system that helps teachers and students set goals and track progress toward them. It also has an instructional coaching cohort dedicated to supporting teachers with modeling, coteaching, coplanning, and classroom-level data analysis.

Bloom's taxonomy is a multitiered model of classifying thinking according to six cognitive levels of complexity. Basically, teachers help students ascend a pyramid using the following steps:

1. Remember
2. Understand
3. Apply
4. Analyze
5. Evaluate
6. Create

I have since visited the classrooms of several teachers using Start Up Math, and the results are pretty exciting. Over and over, we see that kids get excited about business, and that excitement motivates them to improve their math skills because they begin to connect math to the real world. It becomes relevant to their lives.

I visited Amber Harrelson's class at Howard University Middle School of Mathematics and Science, one of the district's highest-performing charter schools. Ms. Harrelson, whose background spans an impressive array of science, technology, engineering, and math (STEM)–based industries, teaches Start Up Math to eight classes of sixth-, seventh-, and eighth-grade students.

She played a fascinating game with the students called Assembly Line. She broke the students into two lines, and each line passed down tennis balls (which were supposed to represent a product) hand to hand to see how many could go through the assembly line in two minutes. The first time both lines had seven students, and one line was able to move sixteen and the other line fourteen tennis balls. She then pretended to lay off two employees from each line, leaving each with five students.

She guided the two groups through creating an income statement to determine how much gross profit would be earned by each line, and subtracting labor and material costs. The kids got so caught up in their "businesses" that they were eager to learn and use percentages and decimals in order to calculate their net profits, return on sales, return on investment, and other information that can be gleaned from an income statement using basic math skills.

I also visited Jefferson Academy and observed Lincoln Campbell, who teaches entrepreneurship and engineering to junior-high students. She used a lesson on marketing research to focus her class on analyzing marketing differences between Takis and Hot Cheetos. She embedded a lesson on percentage and decimals as she led her students through analyzing the demographics, psychographics, and marketing strategies of both brands.

It was a fully integrated entrepreneurship-math class. Campbell used the integration of market research and mathematics concepts to teach Venn diagrams, cost per unit, and budgeting—and her students were very enthusiastic! Afterward I interviewed two students, Ajani and Aymee. They both had business ideas and were eager to start writing their business plans.

Measuring Results

Start Up Math is built around a comprehensive data system that seeks to measure student progress toward mastery of the seventh-grade Common Core standards. Students in Start Up Math are required to take a diagnostic assessment, three formative assessments, and ultimately a summative assessment.

The first sets of data are promising, and NFTE is cautiously optimistic about the program's ability to teach basic mathematics concepts to students while illuminating relevancy in learning.

A preliminary analysis of Start Up Math's impact on student achievement reveals that, collectively, schools using Start Up Math as a stand-alone mathematics class showed an average of 32.5 percent increases between the diagnostic assessment and the first formative assessment. Schools using Start Up Math with 100 percent special-education populations demonstrated an average of 19 percent increases between the diagnostic assessment and the first formative assessment.

One school using Start Up Math had substantial math gains for semester one. At the beginning of the school year, students scored 21 percent and 26 percent on two tested math standards related to unit rates, ratios, and proportions. Since implementing Start Up Math, students are closer to 65 percent mastery in these two mathematics standards.

Start Up Math will evolve as a project-based mathematics option for students struggling with mathematics content, especially as we seek to more seamlessly integrate the math concepts with the business concepts. Next, in conjunction with the NFTE DC Board of Advisors, we plan to identify a comparative group to obtain more data on Start Up Math's success. We are also reaching out to several research and STEM-based organizations as potential partners in order to further improve Start Up Math's design.

Let's Help Our Teachers Teach

It's been one of the great privileges of my life to sit at the feet of great teachers—starting with my mother, who was a beloved special-education teacher—and learn the secrets of bringing young minds to understanding. For all the theories and debates about teaching, it comes down in the end to one person excited by knowledge sharing that knowledge with someone made eager to hear it. If we can get our kids excited about improving their math skills by bringing business lessons into our schools, why not do it?

CHAPTER 6

The Digital Revolution

Technology Levels the Global Playing Field

F OR THE Entrepreneurship Revolution, technology isn't so much a game changer as a field leveler. It gives poor and once-isolated people access to the same information as the rich and fortunate. It breaks down barriers that have held back too many for too long simply because they didn't know that opportunities existed, or that a world of people and institutions was ready to help them.

When I was invited to Russia in the late 1980s to discuss my ideas on teaching entrepreneurship, the political debates were often unsatisfactory and shallow. It was painfully clear that many Russians I met simply didn't have access to information about other economic and political systems that could have helped them break through their ideological upbringings. They may as well have lived on the moon.

In sharp contrast, when I was invited to Cambodia a quarter-century later, the spread of information via the Web was dramatically wider—despite ongoing government censorship of the Cambodian Internet. The government proactively blocks blogs and websites, either on moral grounds or for hosting content deemed critical of the government.

Nonetheless, even though Cambodia had also suffered terribly from communism, the Cambodian people I met were infinitely more aware of alternatives to communism and socialism than the Russians I had met in the 1980s. I believe that's why Cambodia is experiencing such an incredible boom in entrepreneurship and is recovering steadily from the horrors of totalitarianism and genocide it experienced in the 1970s at the hands of the Khmer Rouge.

Entrepreneurs Benefit from Connectivity

Not everything online is good, but it is very hard for bad ideas or wrong notions to survive for long in today's hyperconnected world. Wikipedia crowdsources research in order to post and refine a body of knowledge far bigger than the largest encyclopedias in human history. Old-time gatekeepers—political leaders, financiers, elite journalists—who once defined what was good for the public at large are scrutinized by a global army of bloggers, fact checkers, and critics.

The Digital Revolution is creating new entrepreneurship networks, unlike the exclusive insider networks of the past that were designed to keep wealth and privilege among a favored few.

Today, even the seminomadic Maasai tribespeople of Kenya and northern Tanzania have cell phones. They use them, in fact, to help run their cattle trading business!

According to a fascinating 2010 report by Roela Santos on the Georgetown University Global Communications blog,

> The Kenyan government is leveraging mobile devices to help the Maasai cope with one of Kenya's worst droughts in history. With the help of mobile devices and information shared by researchers, herders can find out where to bring their cattle instead of roaming hundreds of miles in search of water and pasture. The Maasai recharge their phones using solar panels

provided by the government or diesel generators. The Maasai also use their phones to trade and find the best deals when selling or trading cattle.

If You Understand Business Basics, You Can Handle Change

Today's young entrepreneurs are hoping to make their fortune in fields that didn't even exist when I started teaching, such as website design, app creation, database administration, and cybersecurity. Despite the dot-com bust of the late 1990s, great fortunes are being made in the technology field every day, creating spinoff opportunities for entrepreneurs from Boston to Bangalore.

I can see the productivity gains from technology in my own life. It used to take me ten hours of classroom time to teach kids the basics of an income statement; now with the Internet, iPads, and teaching apps, I can go anywhere in the world and do it in an hour. I haven't gotten any smarter, but my productivity has soared. Through discussion groups and message boards, hundreds of NFTE-trained instructors can share tips and pass along best practices, virtually in real time. It is certainly a revolution in how we teach entrepreneurship.

Yet business basics endure. If my kids from 1981 could be transported to the world of today, they would be awed and blown away—for a little while. Back then, my students had to transcend many boundaries—including race and class—to be successful in their businesses. They had to learn a new language—financial literacy—in order to talk with sponsors, suppliers, and potential business partners. They had to learn to explain their business idea in an instant to complete strangers, as well as anticipate any questions or particular concerns potential investors might have.

And because they learned their business basics, they would be able to talk to today's entrepreneurship students about comparative advantages, marketing strategies, customer service, the economics of one unit, and the importance of a business plan. Given a little time to adjust, they would have fit right in and started some exciting new businesses. And they would know how to pitch their new businesses to investors and mentors.

That's the advantage of entrepreneurship education: It gives you the knowledge and skills to not only handle change but to make the most of it.

Internet Speeds Up Creative Destruction

Is there any downside to the Internet revolution, which has put companies and entire industries, from booksellers to travel agents, out of business or in precarious positions? Actually, economists argue that this kind of "creative destruction" is a good thing. Entrepreneurs have always used technology to create new businesses and this, in turn, sometimes causes social disruption.

One of Austrian American economist Joseph Schumpeter's favorite examples of this capitalist phenomenon was the building of transcontinental railroads in the nineteenth century, which led to booms in cities along key routes but destroyed cities not so favorably situated. Schumpeter, who was born in Austria in 1883, argued that the entrepreneur was the hero of the economy, because the entrepreneur disrupts the status quo and causes economic development in new areas.

The Digital Revolution does have the power to speed up and intensify trends in ways that we are still coming to understand. Market bubbles have been an economic fact of life since the birth of capitalism, but the stunning speed with which the 1990s dot-com bubble inflated and burst was still something to behold. Money always flows into new technologies, and the Internet has made the flow particularly frictionless. Entrepreneurs get blamed for the spectacular failures—remember GeoCities and the sock puppet from Pets.com?—but what we were really seeing, in my opinion, was the "cluster of errors" resulting from market enthusiasm, government policy, and cheap money that Mises warned about a century ago.

Less Capital Needed to Start Internet-Based Business

The Internet has been overwhelmingly positive for entrepreneurs as a source of inspiration, a repository of knowledge, and an avenue for marketing, financing, customer feedback, sales, and networking. The Internet-based business model also places far fewer hurdles in the way of an energetic young entrepreneur willing to invest sweat equity. The start-up costs of an Internet business like Instagram are trivial compared to the start-up costs Henry Ford faced a century ago when he was trying to get his assembly-line car manufacturing business up and running.

Internet Impact on Fear of Failure

The Web has spawned some great success stories, but the cyber-community can be equally harsh on those who fall short. With Facebook, Twitter, and other social media efficiently spreading the news, budding business owners aren't allowed to fail in quiet dignity any more—particularly if they relied on the Web to spread the news of their new business in the first place.

As is well known, Thomas Edison finally hit on the right method for making a long-lasting incandescent lightbulb after a lengthy trial-and-error process. Asked by a reporter what it felt like to "fail" so many times before finally getting it right, Edison famously replied, "Young man, I have not failed 999 times. I simply found 999 ways not to make a lightbulb."

The freedom to fail is essential to innovation and entrepreneurship. The very openness and connectivity the Internet provides makes it tough to fail in private, which means that it's even more important that nations encourage entrepreneurial mindsets, including the idea that failing is part of every success. The destigmatization of failure must be a core value of any nation seeking to encourage entrepreneurship.

The Internet and Intellectual Property

Here's another challenge of the Digital Revolution: Try explaining intellectual property (IP) ownership to young people who have been downloading pirated movies and music since they first encountered computers. For that matter, try explaining intellectual property to kids in countries where IP rights enforcement is spotty, to say the least.

There are essentially two IP issues in youth entrepreneurship:

1. How does a young person learn to protect an idea in order to be able to monetize it?
2. How can intellectual property protection be simplified so that it is affordable for the young entrepreneur?

We must make sure our young entrepreneurs understand the four pillars of IP: copyright, trademark, patents, and trade secrets. How can we make young people understand that in order to protect and monetize their own ideas, they must learn to respect the IP rights of others? Complicating this issue is the fact that schools tend to allow students to use music and other materials in film, electronic music classes, and so on, without discussing intellectual property rights at all. Granted, fair use and the TEACH Act allow this type of educational use, but because our schools tend to shy away from business discussion in the classroom, rarely do our children learn these finer points of IP. They just become used to downloading whatever they need for their projects without any thought given to ownership issues.

As for the second question, can we streamline the process for young entrepreneurs so that their rights can be protected with minimal help from a lawyer, for example? Perhaps we could get pro bono IP lawyers to work with our low-income youth to help them protect and be able to monetize their ideas.

A national effort to help young entrepreneurs gain access to lawyers who specialize in IP issues is emerging as an important strategy for the improvement of youth entrepreneurship education. These lawyers have been instrumental both in advising students on their current businesses and creating instructional case studies to help students internalize the advice for the future as well.

Another problem confronting our field involves the group businesses that young people often start within youth entrepreneurship education programs. Many businesses in youth entrepreneurship are based on a group model. The benefits are enormous: kids learn to work in groups, and teamwork skills improve. But creating a business within a team raises sticky legal issues: Who owns a group business? How does ownership transfer?

These issues become compounded when considering them alongside the general attitudes and behaviors of adolescents. Jason Delgatto, a program manager with the NFTE Chicago program office finds that:

Some students create businesses with their best friends, regardless of whether these other students may be the most reliable or trustworthy of business partners. For the groups that may eventually have a falling out, it can be the ultimate learning experience—which of course is better than learning the same lesson later in life when they are more established. However, what many of these students do not realize is the implications of IP ownership in such a split. We have seen some potentially viable businesses and groups deteriorate, simply because some students felt they deserved more because of the disproportionate work they put in, and the terms of ownership were not explicitly discussed in advance.

Equal Ownership Group Business Model

To solve this issue I recommend that youth entrepreneurship educators begin using what I've named the Equal Ownership Group Business model. Essentially, each team business would start out with equal ownership granted to each founder. This model is based on the way Fairchild Semiconductor was set up by legendary venture capitalist Arthur Rock in 1957, in San Francisco's southern Bay Area. Fairchild Semiconductors was one of the first great venture capital deals. Each of the eight scientists who were founders received equal percentages of the business, with the venture capitalists receiving the balance.

The new company produced transistors, selling their first one hundred to IBM at $150 apiece. Two years later, Fairchild researchers invented the integrated microchip. The company grew from twelve to twelve thousand employees and was soon raking in some $130 million a year. Many of the Fairchild founders formed other companies, helping to create Silicon Valley.

If we apply the Fairchild model to a youth group business, a team business with five members would split the business five ways. Each team member would receive a 20 percent equity stake in the business.

In some ways this model would also be similar to the employee stock ownership plan (ESOP) pioneered by Louis Kelso in 1956. In an ESOP, each employee owns part of the company, and when retiring or leaving the business, each person receives a certain amount of money for his or her shares.

Perhaps we could set up youth enterprises so that once a team member reaches age eighteen, the team member could sell his or her shares to the other team members. If a child leaves the business before age eighteen, the other team members could split and share that child's portion of the business equity at a predetermined price—much like a cooperative ownership model works. After young entrepreneurs in the business reach age eighteen, they could negotiate valuations among themselves.

Not only would this approach set fair and concrete guidelines for group ownership for entrepreneurship students to follow, but it would provide tremendous real-life learning opportunities as well. I'd like to see Equal Ownership Group Businesses set up boards, with bylaws and regular meetings, and each team member receiving one vote per share. What a great educational experience it would be for our young entrepreneurs from low-income communities to learn how company boards work!

Next, our team of young entrepreneurs could seek help from

some pro bono IP lawyers to protect any intellectual property the group business generates—from its logo and tagline to inventions. This approach would add enormous value to the business model and make the valuation of the business much easier not only to teach but also calculate.

The team could then use its protected intellectual property, plus a detailed business plan with financial projections, to raise money from investors for their business.

These issues are very advanced in youth entrepreneurship, and no one has ever solved them on a global basis before, but if we do, the world will be a better place for it. Solving these issues will enable the growing field of youth entrepreneurship to lead the way for teaching at-risk youth around the world the very principles of ownership and intellectual property that they can use to discover their own pathways out of poverty.

GenTech: Preparing Young Entrepreneurs to Compete in Tech

With growing opportunities in the tech industry, no wonder many young entrepreneurs are excited about starting businesses in this sector. But while America's educators scramble to beef up STEM (science, technology, engineering, and math) education, a striking disconnect remains between our students' credentials and the training in coding and computer languages necessary to compete in technology—particularly in low-income school districts.

That is why NFTE has partnered with the New York City Economic Development Corporation (NYCEDC) to create NYC Generation Tech (GenTech), a program that seeks to educate and inspire high-school students from low-income communities to pursue careers in entrepreneurship and technology by providing hands-on learning experiences and mentorship opportunities.

In a two-week tech-entrepreneurship "boot camp," students learn the fundamentals of entrepreneurship; develop basic knowledge of HTML, CSS, and JavaScript; and form teams to develop a mobile app and business plan aimed at improving education or the quality of city life for New York City students. During the boot camp, students receive mentorship from undergraduate and graduate students pursuing degrees in business and technology.

Following the boot camp, students continue to develop their coding skills while building out their apps and business plans during weekly classroom sessions and twice-weekly evening mentoring sessions. Each student team is paired with a small team of tech mentors from industry-leading tech and business organizations. Tech mentors provide support, insight, and guidance to students during evening mentoring sessions. Mentoring sessions are held at various tech-related companies throughout New York City.

Finally, students demonstrate and pitch their finished apps and business plans to a panel of prominent judges from the technology, venture capital, and educational communities. Members of the winning team receive cash prizes, and all students are honored at an awards ceremony. Judges have included senior leaders from Tumblr, Microsoft, New York Angels, FirstMark Capital, Birchbox, and Next Generation Broadband.

We also hold the GenTech Hackathon—a tech entrepreneurship competition grouping high-school coders, ranging from novice to expert—for an afternoon so that they can dream up a digital product that benefits their community and build it. The students have a lot of fun while they gain more experience working with tech professionals and building a network of mentors and contacts within the tech and start-up sectors.

The Power of Combining Tech and Entrepreneurship Skills

GenTech programs could help close the huge skills gap in preparing students to compete for jobs and business opportunities in the STEM sectors. GenTech teaches both hard skills like coding and soft skills like public speaking that students need as well. At GenTech, not only do students learn to code, they also receive entrepreneurship training so that they can employ their newly learned skills to create businesses or be successful employees.

All of these factors feed an entrepreneurial spirit in GenTech's students, helping them build confidence, competence, and camaraderie. The mentorships also provide extended support, which aids the students when they apply to college and encourages them to develop employable skills and traits.

In the summer of 2013, participating students spent eleven weeks mastering coding and receiving an intensive introduction to the tech world. They were split into teams of four or five students each and tasked with creating a functional mobile app prototype and business plan based on an idea that would improve the lives of New York City youth. Teams received guidance from tech mentors, who met twice a week with the students at the offices of Google, Warby Parker, and AlleyNYC.

On September 19, the three finalist teams competed at the final Demo Night, sponsored by Microsoft, MasterCard Worldwide, and Verizon Foundation. It was set up just like real demo nights for tech entrepreneurs. The finalist teams had six minutes to pitch their business idea and demo their app. Multiple projection screens showcased their pitches to a packed audience at AppNexus, yet the high-school students were unfazed. In fact, I heard from seasoned members of the tech community that the fourteen- to eighteen-year-olds pitched like pros.

The winning team designed SproutEd, an education network that brings the classroom experience to mobile devices, empowering students to collaborate with peers and discuss school-related topics and events. The team won the opportunity to pitch their mobile app to one of the heaviest hitters in venture capital, Andy Weissman, partner at Union Square Ventures (USV), the firm that helped launch transformative web properties such as Twitter, Tumblr, SoundCloud, and Kickstarter. While listening to entrepreneurs pitch their ideas is nothing out of the ordinary for Weissman, this was the first time he heard a pitch from entrepreneurs who were still in high school.

SproutEd's operation officer Melverton Hunter said, "GenTech changed the way I think in many ways. . . . I actually have the chance to create my own business. When I was younger, I never thought I would have the skills to create a business, but with the skills GenTech gave me, I believe that I can be a technological mogul. Generation Tech opened many doors for me, and I can't wait to see what's next."

After demoing their app and presenting their business plan, the SproutEd team sat down for an open discussion with Weissman and USV analyst Brian Watson. Weissman and Watson provided the team with helpful advice on how to grow a user base and encouraged them to bring their app to market as quickly as possible. The app is slated to be released on Google Play.

Power of Teamwork: Pixlee

When young people learn to work in teams, as GenTech encourages them to do, amazing things can happen. NFTE alum Kyle Wong has raised over \$1.5 million in seed funding and partnered with over seventy-five companies as the cofounder and CEO of Pixlee, a tech company that leverages the trove of visual brand endorsements available on the Web today. Wong has developed a team of fifteen people, including several talented engineers and a seasoned tech executive with deep expertise in rich media.

Pixlee is capitalizing on the behavior of millions of people, especially Millennials, who share hashtagged photos of their favorite teams, stores, and products on social media on a regular basis. Pixlee helps brands see this opportunity to better connect with consumers, using authentic user photos from social media sites as endorsement and marketing channels for big-name companies unlike it's ever been done before. Wong and Pixlee are changing the game for e-commerce companies, lifestyle businesses, sporting and sponsored events, live performances, and travel.

I interviewed Wong about the importance of teamwork to his success.

STEVE MARIOTTI: Can you explain what your company does?
KYLE WONG: By using Pixlee, companies no longer need to hire models to pose with their product, searching for a way to reach out to their target demographic. Regular people who drink Coke or wear The North Face—just two of Pixlee's big-name clients— hashtag photos and get featured on the company's site. For Coke and The North Face this means more exposure, better market-

ing, and ultimately increased conversion and engagement for the company.

SM: As a young company, what was your strategy in building your team?

KW: We pride ourselves on having some of the best engineers and designers in Silicon Valley. We think a great engineering team leads to a great product, and a great product leads to happy customers. We also believe in building a "full-stack" team with complementary skill sets both on the engineering and business team. By having a nice combination of experience and talent on both teams, we think we have a great foundation for growth.

SM: What is it like being a young entrepreneur, and how do you play off the strengths of your teammates?

KW: It's always beneficial as an entrepreneur to have insights on the space that you're entering. While the founders don't have a formal marketing background, prior to Pixlee we have created businesses that are directly related to this space. When it comes to user-generated photos, we understand what has changed in the market because our friends and age group are the ones who are led to the massive growth in photo sharing.

Through Pixlee, Kyle Wong and his cofounders—Awad Sayeed, Miraj Mohsin, and Jeff Chen—are changing the way customers and companies connect. Their ideas are disrupting traditional marketing, potentially making it more customized, intimate, and personal. And they developed these ideas because, as young social media users themselves, they have unique knowledge of their market.

But without exposure to entrepreneurship education, the Digital Revolution and all its fantastic opportunities might have passed these young people by. In this sense, my field hasn't changed a bit over the years. The mission of entrepreneurship education is still to help the young and at-risk to organize and expand the mental map of their own possibilities.

For all the increases in computing speed, connectivity, and artificial intelligence, the ultimate technological marvel, in my opinion, remains the gray matter inside a young person's head. It hosts unlimited potential to change our world for the better.

CHAPTER 7

On the Cusp

A Financing Revolution

W E'RE ON THE cusp of a golden age of entrepreneurship financing. The Entrepreneurship Revolution has the potential to lift so many of the world's people out of poverty— and the Digital Revolution is helping new entrepreneurs find the financing they need to launch their businesses.

Because of the Digital Revolution, a low-income entrepreneur in a developing country can interact with financial backers through a microcredit platform like Kiva. A young entrepreneur can crowdfund a start-up with Indiegogo or Fundable. A small business can get a loan to grow through a peer-to-peer lending platform like The Lending Club. The Financing Revolution is another big reason I am such an optimist about how entrepreneurs will change the world over the next one hundred years. Every year we get smarter at financing entrepreneurship and encouraging ownership at the margins.

Personal assets, money from friends, bank or government lending, and venture capital once defined the universe of choices for start-up cash. When those sources dried up during the Great Recession, entrepreneurs had to get more creative about financing than ever. The small businesses that survived the Great Recession have faced severe challenges acquiring capital to expand their businesses to thrive in today's recovering economy.

Access to capital continues to remain more limited for entrepreneurs that it should be for optimum economic growth worldwide. Luckily crowdfunding, microfinance, and peer-to-peer lending are providing critical financing for grassroots microbusinesses, as well as for small businesses in the five hundred employees or fewer range. It's still tough for many worthy businesses to obtain financing—the golden age isn't here quite yet—but these creative new financing methods are definitely revolutionary.

Louis Kelso: Leveling the Playing Field

I want to share an incident I consider one of the greatest privileges I've had since founding NFTE. It was 1989 at the Grand Hyatt Hotel in San Francisco. Accompanied by eleven wide-eyed NFTE students I was able to talk with the great economist and investor Louis Kelso just two years before his death. Kelso, who in addition to his pioneering work on economic theory also founded Kelco & Company—a merchant bank that now ranks among the fifty largest private equity firms in the world, was a thoroughgoing realist about the workings of the market. The old Roman gladiatorial arena, he once famously remarked, "was technically a level playing field. . . . But on one side were lions with all the weapons, and on the other the Christians with all the blood. That's not a level playing field; that's a slaughter. And so is putting people into the economy without equipping them with capital, while equipping a tiny handful of people with hundreds of thousands of times more than they can use."

Kelso argued that someone who is born without capital—and capital can be defined in a wide variety of ways, from money and reputation to knowledge, people, skills, and intellectual property—should not be denied a chance for ownership of the means of production. With his revolutionary work on employee stock ownership plans and consumer stock ownership plans, Kelso did more to aid the "Christians" of the economic world than perhaps any thinker before or since. His 1958 book, *The Capitalist Manifesto*, is a classic that everyone in economic development should read.

Even though Kelso was clearly ailing when we met, he generously spent six hours patiently answering the many questions our kids asked him. We tried after that meeting to apply his groundbreaking ideas on profit sharing and employee ownership to enterprises run by NFTE, and though we ran into some technical hurdles, his generosity and insights remain an inspiration for our work to this day.

Most striking to me was that Kelso used the principles of capitalism to address some of the problems caused by capitalism. Through his work and the work of others, we are coming ever closer to the day when everyone can benefit from the power of markets and the dynamism of entrepreneurship, empowering workers as well as owners. That will be the greatest financial revolution of all time.

Harnessing Crowd Power

I think Kelso would have been thrilled by innovations like crowdfunding. Crowdfunding involves persuading many individuals to fund a project with small donations—typically in exchange for a reward or perk. A donation might be as small as one dollar in exchange for a free music download or as large as one thousand dollars in exchange for tickets to attend a red-carpet movie premiere (one of the rewards for the *Veronica Mars* campaign). The more donors, the more cash you raise. If you attract thousands of donors, you could raise some serious cash.

When Rob Thomas, creator of the popular television series *Veronica Mars*, couldn't get a budget from Warner Bros. to make a *Veronica Mars* feature film, he turned to the crowdfunding site Kickstarter. Thomas raised $2 million on Kickstarter in ten hours. By the end of the campaign, he had raised $5.7 million, along with tons of publicity and invested fans.

The movie cost $6 million to make and earned $2 million in its first weekend during a limited theatrical release. It was also released as video on demand (VOD), where it was estimated to have earned another $1 million that weekend. Box Office Mojo has reported that the film's box office was $3.49 million worldwide, and another $4 million in domestic DVD sales. Not too shabby.

Crowdsourcing has tossed the traditional method of trying to raise financing—from wealthy individuals or big corporations like Warner Bros.—on its ear. That is a godsend for entrepreneurs.

Typically, the crowdfunding platform just takes a cut of the money you raise. Kickstarter collects 5 percent and uses the all-or-nothing model—if you fail to raise the amount stated as your campaign goal, you do not get any money. Indiegogo takes 4 percent if you raise your stated campaign goal and 9 percent if you do not. Either way, on Indiegogo you get to keep the money you raise.

Financial Fear Is Debilitating

Being able to raise financing for a small business can mean the difference between living with poverty and constant financial fear or moving forward toward peace of mind and security. Financial fear is debilitating. It can shut the body down, disrupt one's ability to concentrate on work, and demolish relationships.

As a teacher of at-risk youth for three decades and a specialist in dropout prevention at the high-school and junior-high levels, I dealt with many students who could not focus. As I came to know them I discovered that my most insubordinate and disruptive students were typically living with serious financial worry and anxiety.

Academic achievement is far more difficult for a chronically anxious and fearful child. I witnessed so many of my students gain confidence and self-esteem and improve their academic performance when they began earning even small sums of money through their little businesses. Being able to do so gave them hope and made them feel less disempowered and disenfranchised.

I also speak from personal experience, for there wasn't a day during the first decade that we were trying to get NFTE off the ground that I wasn't very worried about financing. My first two applications for a Small Business Innovation Research grant were rejected before we won a lifesaving fifty-thousand-dollar grant in 1986.

We were still desperate for funding, however. As a last resort I sat down with the *Forbes* 400 list and wrote a letter to each person on it. One wrote back, and a thirty-minute meeting with Ray Chambers at his Morristown, New Jersey, office in 1987 produced the two-hundred-thousand-dollar investment that enabled NFTE to truly begin fulfilling our mission. If we could have freed up just a fraction of the time I spent worrying about funding to concentrate on the core work that NFTE was supposed to be doing, however, we could have helped so many more kids far more quickly.

Today, a start-up nonprofit has many financing options to explore. Crowdfunding for social causes is quickly gaining in popularity. Sites like Crowdrise, Razoo, and StartSome Good are redefining how nonprofits and social enterprises raise money for events and charitable causes.

Entrepreneurship Is Financially Risky

Let's be honest, though. Being an entrepreneur is inherently financially stressful. Business failure can exacerbate poverty. Being able to buy low and sell high—the entrepreneur's mantra—is never guaranteed. A product can drop in value before it is sold. It may be stolen or sit in a warehouse because demand is low. A desirable product may never take off because the right consumers never hear about it.

Entrepreneurs must be time travelers because entrepreneurship involves attempting to forecast a future that is unknowable and meeting future needs by investing time, energy, and scarce resources. The entrepreneur is never completely sure of consumer needs or what competitors are doing. Entrepreneurs must trust their guts and make educated guesses.

An entrepreneur who makes good decisions is rewarded with profit. Entrepreneurs who are making profits improve society by disrupting monopolies and lowering prices, introducing new products and services and improving old ones. Entrepreneurs who are earning profits can hire people; they add to society's capital and move us all toward the future. They solve problems, unite diverse people, and improve the allocation of scarce resources.

A successful entrepreneur has to be a lifelong researcher— of product niches, of innovations in production and service, of new ways to obtain financing and other support, of evolving best practices in the field, and of the tastes and needs of customers now and in the future.

Conversely, when an entrepreneur loses money by, for example, only being able to sell for forty dollars something that cost fifty dollars to produce, he has subtracted ten dollars from society. A growing economy is one in which entrepreneurs are making profits and expanding their businesses; a recession is when they, as a community, are making mistakes and losing money.

LEARNING TO HANDLE FINANCIAL UNCERTAINTY IS A SKILL

Precisely because entrepreneurship is financially risky I believe every child on the planet should experience ownership. Starting and running a small business with the support of an entrepreneurship education program teaches young people to deal constructively with financial risk and uncertainty and the accompanying emotional stress. It teaches them to accept responsibility for their choices and inspires them to believe in themselves, even when they fail. They learn that tweaking a business idea or marketing it differently can change it from unsuccessful to successful. They learn that, as Robert F. Kenney famously said, "Only those who dare to fail greatly can ever achieve greatly."

Learning to handle financial uncertainty is a skill, and skills can be taught. Yes, the paralysis of financial fear can be life-destroying. But fear can also create a heightened sense of awareness, be a motivator, and instill the determination that leads to success. Entrepreneurship education produces empowered young entrepreneurs who can live with the fear of the unknown because they have the real-life experience and tools to master it.

Once an individual learns how to cope with—rather than

avoid—financial uncertainty, it changes that person forever. Students who learn basic accounting and how to create a cash flow statement are forever less likely to hide their heads in the sand or act out in counterproductive ways when it comes to financial matters. They know how much cash they have, and they know how to make more. They start to take responsibility for their financial lives. The future begins to seem full of possibility.

The earlier young people are exposed to new ideas and learn new skills, the greater impact these will have on their adult lives. Young people exposed to entrepreneurship develop financial awareness and are better able to cope with the inevitable stresses that come with earning and managing money later in life. Exposing young people to entrepreneurship is a valuable strategy to prepare them for an uncertain world. In doing so, we will create a community of entrepreneurs who can solve problems and create wealth and jobs. And that will help us all.

Here are six things NFTE seeks to teach every student regarding financial risk and uncertainty:

1. *Always know how much money you have.* Keep a daily cash flow statement and a monthly balance sheet. Financial fear can motivate you to create a new world. To do that you must first be aware of your assets, liabilities, and equity. A balance sheet shows you what they are.
2. *Make a budget* to show how much you are spending and on what. This will help you feel in control of your financial life.
3. *Establish financial goals* so that you can visualize not only where you are but where you need to be.
4. *Be open about fear and stress.* You are only as weak as your secrets, so get your fears into the open.

5. *Save at least 10 percent of everything you earn.* Invest early to create wealth. Time is on your side!
6. *Learn to recognize others' needs and problems as business opportunities.* Sometimes these needs will be based on fear, which you have embraced and studied.

Crowdfunding Surges

If you've ever watched *Shark Tank*, you know the true measure of the commitment an entrepreneur makes to a business is how much money he or she has been sunk into it. And you've also seen the tap dancing that entrepreneurs have to do in front of venture capitalists. Venture capital and the expertise and networks that venture capitalists bring to a business can be huge game changers, but gaining access to venture capital is pretty tough, and the entrepreneur who does attract venture capital must be very careful not to give away the (equity) farm in exchange for financing.

In reality, according to Small Business Administration data, more than 60 percent of all start-ups tap personal savings, borrow against personal assets, and use credit cards to get their businesses up and running. Crowdfunding is surging forward also as an exciting new way for entrepreneurs to obtain financing—without giving away chunks of equity. According to a survey by the consulting firm Massolution of over 360 crowdsourcing platforms, around $5.1 billion in transactions occurred globally in 2013. That's around a 100 percent increase from 2012 when $2.7 billion was raised.

Equity Crowdfunding Gets a Boost from Obama

Prior to 2012, equity crowdfunding was a relatively tiny slice of the pie. While federal regulators struggle to get their hands around the online-based financing mechanism, only accredited investors could make direct investments in start-ups using crowdsourced funds.

Equity crowdfunding got a boost, however, when President Obama signed the Jumpstart Our Business Startups (JOBS) Act into law on April 5, 2012. Raising capital is strictly regulated by the Securities and Exchanges Commission, but the JOBS Act provided new exemptions for the use of Internet funding portals that enable small businesses to use crowdfunding to raise money.

And the crowdfunding industry, like the Internet itself, is proving to be highly adaptable. Prominent businesses that received crowdsourced early funding boosts include the smartphone Ubuntu Edge, the "smartwatch" Pebble, and Star Citizen, a top video game. Some Web-based funding platforms, such as Fundraise.com, CauseVox, and Fundly have carved out a niche targeting nonprofits.

Using Crowdfunding to Build Credibility

Entrepreneurs are also using crowdfunding to build credibility in the marketplace before they seek more traditional forms of equity financing. When Marisol Trowbridge started Puzzle Apparel, a company that sells customized garments manufactured in Brooklyn using handmade fabrics from American artists, she felt it was too early to take the concept to angels or venture capitalists. Instead, Trowbridge started a monthlong campaign on Indiegogo. She wanted to raise $10,000 to pay for production and prove market interest; a month later, she had raised $10,193.

Trowbridge told *Crain's New York Business* ("Crowdfunding Helps Women Beat Financing Odds" by Eileen Zimmerman,

February 5, 2014) that as a female entrepreneur, she feels she must back up her ideas with proof they work in order to be taken seriously, but she also believes that doing so is a smart business practice for any entrepreneur. "This isn't just a male-female issue, but an issue of letting the market lead you," Trowbridge noted.

Caron Proschan, cofounder of Manhattan-based Simply Gum, an all-natural chewing gum that launched in October 2013, also used crowdfunding to establish her product's viability before seeking investment capital. After raising fifteen thousand dollars on Kickstarter in June 2013, Proschan went on to raise a seed round from investors that October.

Proschan told Crain's that for her the process was "almost less about funding than about consumer feedback. People are very vocal in the comment section, and the feedback was overwhelmingly positive. It was more efficient than focus groups and gave us the confidence to go out and find funding from investors."

Female Entrepreneurs Rock Nontraditional Financing

Entrepreneurship has proven to be an effective way for minorities and women to enter the business world—and the financing revolution under way is making it easier. Between 1997 and 2012, when the number of businesses in the United States increased by 37 percent, the number of women-owned firms increased by 54 percent—a rate one and a half times the national average. As of 2012, women own about 40 percent of all private businesses in the United States, according to the Center for Women's Business Research. There are over 8.3 million women-owned

A few crowdfunding mega-success stories:

Formlabs

MIT Media Lab students Maxim Lobovsky, Natan Linder, and David Granor created the first affordable desktop 3D printer, Form 1. After setting a $100,000 goal, they raised nearly $3 million on Kickstarter to launch Formlabs, Inc. in 2011. In 2013, the company received $19 million in venture capital.

TikTok

Chicago designer Scott Wilson's TikTok and LunaTik wristbands, which converted the Apple iPod Nano into a watch, attracted 13,500-plus backers and almost $1 million in funding. He'd asked for just $15,000. TikTok and LunaTik are now sold by Amazon, Walmart, and Apple.

Amanda Palmer's
$1-Million-Plus Music Deal

Amanda Palmer's record deal is the highest funded Kickstarter music project ever, breaking the million-dollar mark for her record, *Art Book*, and tour with the Grand Theft Orchestra. Her original goal of $100,000 was reached within a day.

Diaspora

Diaspora is an open-source social network created by four young programmers from NYU. The students blew through their original $10,000 goal to raise more than $200,000 from 6,479 backers—including Facebook founder Mark Zuckerberg.

businesses in the United States, generating nearly $1.3 trillion in revenues and employing 7,697,000 people.

As mentioned in chapter 6, women have taken to crowdfunding in droves to fund their enterprises. Indiegogo is a popular crowdfunding platform. Of its successful campaigns, 42 percent were run by women. In "Crowdfunding Helps Women Beat Financing Odds," Eileen Zimmerman quoted research from the MIT Sloan School of Management, the Wharton School, and Harvard Business School that has found that men are 40 percent more likely to get venture capital funding with the same pitch as women. Female entrepreneurs are increasingly looking to crowdfunding first—or as a replacement for—venture funding, according to Ethan Mollick, an assistant professor at the University of Pennsylvania's Wharton School of Business who studies gender and equality in entrepreneurship.

"Women have a very difficult time with venture capital," said Mollick. His research shows that women do as well as men on Kickstarter, adding that female entrepreneurs account for between 16 percent and 20 percent of the technology projects on the platform. "For a given project, if it is led by a woman, it will do at least well—if not better—than a similar project proposed by a man," Mollick stated. In total, men raise more money on Kickstarter, but only because more men are running more Kickstarter campaigns.

Minority Entrepreneurs Use Crowdfunding to Level the Playing Field

Census data shows that the growth of minority-owned businesses nationwide has outpaced the average by almost two to

one. From 2002 to 2007 the number of minority-owned businesses grew by 46 percent, to 5.8 million, or more than twice the
rate of businesses as a whole.

The U.S. Small Business Administration reports that 70 percent of all African American–owned start-ups are funded from
personal savings or by family and friends. Most are started with
less than five thousand dollars in up-front costs.

Nonetheless, the credit freeze that has affected most entrepreneurs since the Great Recession has been even icier for minority
small business owners seeking access to capital.

According to the 2012 report "Minority and Immigrant Entrepreneurs: Access to Financial Capital" by economist Robert W.
Fairlie, minority small businesses are less likely to receive small
business loans than nonminority firms and are more likely to
receive lower loan amounts than nonminority firms. In addition, Fairlie uncovered that minorities are charged higher interest rates—even with credit profiles that are equal to those of
nonminority borrowers.

Such discriminatory lending practices damage us all. Fairlie
concluded, "If minority-owned firms would have reached economic parity in 2002, these firms would have employed over
16.1 million workers and grossed over $2.5 trillion in receipts."
Lack of minority access to capital limits the growth of our economy as a whole.

In response to this problem, African Americans and other
minorities are developing new frameworks for investment in
minority start-ups. BlackStartup made its debut in April 2013
with a crowdfunding platform that focuses on funding projects benefiting African Americans. Founders Nathan Bennett-
Fleming, Olugbolahan Adewumi, Aaron O. Brien, Kyle Yeldell,
and Christopher Hollins told NewsOne for Black America that

they are determined to close the "black start-up gap" by fixing the root cause: lack of capital.

In an interview with NewsOne's Hayat Mohamed ("Black-Startup: The African American Solution to Crowdfunding," (May 14, 2013), Bennett-Fleming said, "There is no specific type of businesses that we are attempting to promote. We want to support projects, ideas, and causes that are broadly connected to the African American community."

The site premiered with seven projects, including a math curriculum taught through playing the piano, a family business that makes homemade hair products, and a website featuring social commentary on daily news. BlackStartup won the coveted Yale Entrepreneur Institute's Fellowship, receiving twenty thousand dollars in capital seed money, an elite mentor, and a ten-week boot camp in New Haven.

Although BlackStartup focuses primarily on supporting black causes through funding, Bennett-Fleming says that he and the founders intend to expand to help other marginalized groups. "We are considering broadening our approach to include other minority groups on our platform," he said. "We want to use these new technologies to address the black entrepreneurial gap, the black opportunity gap, and other economic challenges facing the black community as well as other marginalized communities."

BANKING WITHOUT BANKS: PEER-TO-PEER LENDING EXPLODES

Minority entrepreneurs are also partnering with credit unions and community lenders to improve the ability of minority entrepreneurs to qualify for small business loans. The lending side of crowdfunding is also booming. Peer-to-peer lending (also known as person-to-person lending, peer-to-peer investing, and social lending; abbreviated frequently as P2P lending) is the practice of lending money to unrelated individuals, or "peers." Investors provide funding, and borrowers make monthly payments. By cutting out the middleman (banks) and using technology to lower costs, P2P lending platforms are able to lower the cost of credit and pass the savings back in the form of lower rates for borrowers than banks provide and higher returns for investors. Some P2P platforms slice, dice, and package the loans; others allow lenders to pick them. Either way, the result can be a strikingly better deal for both sides.

Investors visiting P2P platforms can browse available notes and screen for certain attributes, such as interest rates, a borrower's debt-to-income ratio, and FICO scores. Lending Club and Prosper—the two biggest U.S. peer-to-peer lending sites—also assign ratings based on the borrower's creditworthiness and the size and length of the loan.

Inside each listing, the borrower describes what he or she plans to use the money for, and potential investors can ask questions. Investors can choose to fund all or just a portion of the loan. After the loan is completely funded, investors will start to receive their share of monthly principal and interest payments.

Loans made via such P2P platforms as Kiva and Prosper hit $1.7 billion in 2012, up from $555 million the year before. Lending Club and Prosper reported that they originated $3 billion in new loans in 2013, up from $870 million in 2012.

At Prosper, borrowers choose a loan amount and purpose and post a loan listing. Investors review loan listings and invest in listings that meet their criteria. Once the process is complete, borrowers make fixed monthly payments, and investors receive a portion of those payments directly to their Prosper account.

In 2014 Lending Club announced its expansion into business loans. The loans will range from fifteen thousand to one hundred thousand dollars initially, increasing to three hundred thousand dollars in the future. Loans carry fixed interest rates that vary with the borrower's creditworthiness. Rates start at 5.9 percent with terms of one to five years, no hidden fees, and no prepayment penalties. The average interest rate on the platform is around 12.5 percent. Lending Club reported making a total $7.6 billion in loans as of January 2015. "Lending Club's platform has the potential to profoundly transform traditional banking over the next decade," says Lending Club board member and former U.S. secretary of the treasury Larry Summers. Lending Club's December 2014 IPO shot to a valuation of $8.5 billion—higher than all but fourteen U.S. banks..

P2P LENDING RISKS

Of course, savvy entrepreneurs know that there is an inverse relationship between risk and reward. The higher returns lenders receive on P2P platforms do indicate higher risk. P2P loans are not federally guaranteed, for example. Although executives for Lending Club and Prosper say well-diversified investors in higher-quality loans rarely lose money, until the companies have been around longer, it's hard to say whether we will see a major collapse of a P2P platform that could take its investors' money down with it.

The platforms say that borrowers will still be required to pay, and backup companies are contracted to take over loan processing in the event of a bankruptcy—but you never know. Another risk is lack of liquidity. It is difficult to get your money back before the loans mature.

Microcredit Platforms

The financing revolution also includes microcredit platforms like Kiva that enable people around the world to provide capital to needy entrepreneurs in developing countries. Kiva works with microfinance institutions on five continents to provide microloans to people without access to traditional banking systems. Microfinance is a general term for financial services provided to people who do not have access to typical banking services.

A microloan is a relatively small amount of money—typically under ten thousand dollars—and generally carries a higher rate of interest than a bank would charge. A microloan can be a lifesaver for a small start-up that doesn't need much capital and has a limited credit history. In the United States, microloans are usually extended to low-income small-business owners by nonprofit organizations through the Small Business Administration. In contrast, through its platform, Kiva links borrowers around the world directly to private lenders.

Microcredit Pros and Cons

The microcredit concept began in Bangladesh with Grameen Bank, founded in 1983 by Muhammad Yunus. Yunus began by using his own money to deliver small loans at low interest rates to the rural poor. He received the Nobel Peace Prize in 2006 for providing microcredit services to the poor. Microcredit became a popular tool for economic development, with hundreds of institutions emerging in the developing world. Ironically many of these early microcredit organizations now function as independent banks. Some have unfortunately been accused of loan sharking; Unit Desa (Village Bank) in Indonesia, for example, has charged in excess of 20 percent on small business loans.

The impact of microcredit depends upon whom you ask, frankly. Proponents like the Consultative Group to Assist the Poor (CGAP), housed at the World Bank, claim that microfinance provides low-income individuals with opportunities to lift themselves out of poverty via entrepreneurship. According to CGAP:

> Comprehensive impact studies have demonstrated that: Microfinance helps very poor households meet basic needs and protect against risks.
>
> The use of financial services by low-income households is associated with improvements in household economic welfare and enterprise stability or growth.
>
> By supporting women's economic participation, microfinance helps to empower women, thus promoting gender-equity and improving household well-being.
>
> For almost all significant impacts, the magnitude of impact is positively related to the length of time that clients have been in the program.

Critics argue that microcredit has not led to increased incomes and has even driven some poor households into debt traps—in some tragic cases even leading to suicide. Heartbreakingly, *Business Insider* reported on February 14, 2012, "Hundreds of Suicides in India Linked to Microfinance Organizations." More than two hundred poor, debt-ridden residents of Andhra Pradesh killed themselves in late 2010, according to media reports compiled by the government of the south Indian state. The state blamed microfinance companies—which give small loans intended to lift up the very poor—for fueling a frenzy of over-indebtedness and then pressuring borrowers so relentlessly that some took their own lives. The companies, including market leader SKS Microfinance, denied it, but internal documents obtained by the Associated Press and an independent investigation confirmed the company's involvement in predatory, threatening tactics that led directly to the suicides.

As Alok Prasad, chief executive of the Microfinance Institutions Network, the industry group that commissioned the investigation, stated, "You come down to a handful of cases where some things went wrong. Is that indicative of the model being bad or very rapid expansion leading to a loss of control?"

Add Entrepreneurship Education to Microfinance

There are two significant issues with microcredit:

1. Predatory lending.
2. Unsustainable debt accumulation by borrowers, which replaces poverty due to deprivation with poverty due to debt.

Another argument is that microloans do not provide enough capital to start a meaningful business. Many billionaire entrepreneurs, however, started with very small capital investments. Dick Schulze started Best Buy with nine thousand dollars. Mark Zuckerberg started Facebook with nothing but his coding talent in his college dorm room.

I believe that recipients of microloans will be both far less vulnerable to predatory lending and unsustainable debt accumulation and also far more likely to be able to grow significant businesses if they receive entrepreneurship education in conjunction with microloans. We can also reduce unhealthy and dangerous dependency on microfinance institutions by helping microborrowers establish credit. United Prosperity, for example, provides a guarantee to a local bank, which then lends back double that amount to the microentrepreneur. This allows the microentrepreneur to develop a credit history.

Microlenders in the United States do teach basic business courses. I'd like to see every microlending platform in the world partner with a provider of entrepreneurship education to do the same. Let's teach borrowers how to run their microbusinesses and grow them into powerhouses—while also becoming financially literate and too savvy to fall prey to predators.

Kiva: Interest-Free Microlending

Kiva's reputation so far is unblemished by the kind of tragic problems that have beset some microcredit operations. What makes Kiva noteworthy is that its lenders do not receive any interest. Using its person-to-person lending model, the delinquency rate (late payment) has been only 3.82 percent, and the default rate (failure to pay) has been just 1.39 percent. Lenders can follow online journals kept by Kiva borrowers.

At Kiva, 100 percent of each loan is sent to microfinance institutions called Field Partners that administer the loans in the field. Kiva relies on a worldwide network of volunteers who work with Field Partners to edit and translate borrower stories and ensure the smooth operation of countless other Kiva programs.

Kiva claims that microfinance can smooth consumption levels and significantly reduce the need to sell assets to meet basic needs. With access to microinsurance, for example, poor people can cope with sudden increased expenses associated with death, serious illness, and loss of assets. CGAP notes the following results:

- Bangladesh Rural Advancement Committee (BRAC) clients increased household expenditures by 28 percent and assets by 112 percent. The incomes of Grameen members were 43 percent higher than incomes in nonprogram villages.
- In El Salvador, the weekly income of Foundation for International Community Assistance (FINCA) clients increased on average by 145 percent.
- In India, half of Self-help and Resource Exchange (SHARE) clients graduated out of poverty.
- In Ghana, 80 percent of clients of Freedom from Hunger had secondary income sources, compared to 50 percent for nonclients.
- In Lombok, Indonesia, the average income of Bank Rakyat Indonesia (BRI) borrowers increased by 112 percent, and 90 percent of households graduated out of poverty.
- In Vietnam, Save the Children clients reduced food deficits from three months to one month.

A number of NFTE graduates have used crowdfunding to get their own businesses off the ground. Twenty-year-old Jennifer, New England's 2013 Young Entrepreneur of the Year, used GoFundMe to obtain financing for her Sugar Coated Heaven shop in Providence, Rhode Island. Another recent grad, D'Anna, used the site to raise money for her college tuition. Jonathan, an NFTE alum who is studying entrepreneurship at college, used Fundly to fund his study-abroad internship in Ireland.

The Lean Start-Up

The lean start-up is another concept revolutionizing entrepreneurship financing. Proposed by Silicon Valley entrepreneur and author Eric Ries in 2008, a lean start-up is a business started with minimal capital and planning that has the flexibility to evolve in response to feedback from customers. Ries argued on his blog, Startup Lessons Learned, that entrepreneurs should launch their business first and plan second. In other words, leap in and adjust as you go!

Zappos, the world's largest online shoe store, did just that. When starting the store, Zappos' Nick Swinmurn simply took pictures of shoes from stores and posted them online. Rather than investing in warehouses and inventory, Swinmurn plunged right in—essentially conducting his market research while already in business. He could quickly see which types of shoes customers wanted, what sizes were most popular, and so on without pouring a lot of money into the business.

Swinmurn created what Ries calls a "façade"—anything that gets your business up and running in front of customers, like a website, for example. He started Zappos with what Ries labels minimum viable product (MVP)—the smallest amount of product needed to begin selling to potential customers. In 2011 Ries published his influential book *The Lean Startup: How Today's Entrepreneurs Use Continuous Innovation to Create Radically Successful Businesses*, which became a *New York Times* best seller.

The deal-of-the-day website Groupon is another fascinating example of a business that got up and running using lean start-up ideas. Groupon founder Andrew Mason started by rapidly assembling a set of deals without a lot of focus on the presentation. He incentivized customers to give rapid feedback so that he could quickly find out which deals were the most popular—and then go out and get more of those deals to sell.

In short, the lean start-up favors getting the business up and running as soon as possible instead of doing a lot of preplanning and using customer feedback to tweak the business. Ries believes that relying on customer feedback during product development ensures that the business does not invest time designing features or services that consumers do not want.

Ries says, "Lean has nothing to do with how much money a company raises." Instead, being lean is about listening to the specific demands of consumers and responding to them rapidly, using the least amount of resources possible.

Intuit, DropBox, Wealthfront, Votizen, Aardvark, and Grockit have all adopted the lean start-up philosophy, and lean start-up classes are taught at Harvard Business School. Even municipal governments in the United States are exploring this approach through Code for America, a nonprofit that connects technology and design professionals with city governments to build open-source applications and promote openness, participation, and efficiency in government.

Rising Tide Capital: Combining Financing and Education

Eight years ago I met a remarkable couple who had married after graduating from Harvard together. In 2004 Alex Forrester and Alfa Demmellash founded Rising Tide Capital, a nonprofit that helps low-income people finance small businesses and provides them with entrepreneurship education. Rising Tide Capital is a real potential game changer for low-income entrepreneurs and the economy as a whole.

Demmellash's difficult childhood in Ethiopia is at the core of her mission. She spent her first twelve years living in Addis Ababa with her aunts while her mother, who had escaped the dictatorship and emigrated to the United States, worked as a waitress and seamstress—hoping to one day bring Alfa to the United States.

When Demmellash was eight years old, her abusive biological father kidnapped her and tortured her for a year before abandoning her in the desert. She walked until she was able to hitch a ride with a trucker back to Addis Ababa, where she found her way back to her family. It took three more years before she was able to join her mother in the United States.

Driven and highly intelligent, Demmellash excelled scholastically and was accepted at Harvard University, where she studied the underlying political, social, and economic dynamics that led to the unrest that had separated her from her mother for so many years. These studies led her to travel to Rwanda in 2002 to study the genocide there and its aftermath.

Months after graduating from Harvard, she and her husband founded Rising Tide Capital in an effort to merge entrepreneurship education and microfinance. They plan to build a replicable model that can be locally adopted in low-wealth communities and used as a catalyst for social and economic empowerment. I interviewed Demmellash in February 2014:

STEVE MARIOTTI: Why have you focused on microbusiness development?

ALFA DEMMELLASH: Since 2004, Rising Tide Capital has witnessed the power of microbusinesses. Whether part time or full time, the businesses that our entrepreneurs have started are changing lives. At first, their businesses represent the ability to meet their families' basic needs—food, clothing, and shelter. Later on, money from a home business might represent the opportunity for social mobility through investments in a home or education. For some of our entrepreneurs who are further along in their journeys, their businesses represent financial independence and the opportunity to influence not just their own lives, but their actual communities.

While microbusinesses employ only five or fewer people, they literally sustain our economy. According to the Association for Enterprise Opportunity, there are 25.5 million microbusinesses in the United States. They employ 31 million people and represent 90 percent of all businesses in the United States.

Microbusinesses are the engine of our local economies and represent our best hope for a healthy national economy. If all U.S. microbusinesses increased their annual revenue by just five thousand dollars a year—less than five hundred dollars a month—more than $20 billion would be generated.

SM: What is your take on microlending?
AD: Microloans—and more importantly the business education and guidance on how to successfully use these loans—have the potential to revitalize our communities. On a local level, a strong microbusiness community means more tax revenue, more jobs, and more dollars circulating in the local economy. It means stronger educational institutions, better local health care, more recreational services, and generally a higher quality of life.

Whether on an individual, local, or national level, the impact of sustainable microbusinesses is real. Rising Tide Capital believes that by reaching individuals who have not been exposed to the types of programs we offer, we can empower them to create their own opportunities.

The Community Business Academy (CBA) is the signature program of Rising Tide Capital. It consists of twelve consecutive three-hour sessions. The classes are conveniently held once a week on weekday evenings or Saturday mornings. Sessions run twice per year from February through May and from September through December. Entrepreneurs are taught business fundamentals like budgeting, marketing, bookkeeping, and financing. Every applicant accepted into the CBA receives a full tuition waiver (worth three thousand dollars), thanks to the generosity of Rising Tide Capital's funding partners. Graduates of the Community Business Academy become part of Rising Tide Capital's alumni network and continue to receive ongoing support as they work on their businesses.

Imagine the potential improvement in our economy if every community in our nation had a Community Business Academy. Imagine how many new entrepreneurs would be minted and how many people saved from lives of financial desperation, or, even crime. As Alfa explains so eloquently, strong local economies add up to a strong national economy and a strong nation.

What are we waiting for?

CHAPTER 8

A Prison Revolution

Desperately Needed

THE POWER of entrepreneurship education to change a prisoner's life has long been a special passion of mine. NFTE regularly donates our entrepreneurship books to prisons, and as a result I have received over ten thousand letters from prisoners over the last twenty years, all asking for advice on how to start a business. I've personally witnessed many urban youth choose a legal business career over the drug trade once they became financially literate. I've seen them, with a little help, start and run successful businesses, put themselves through college, and find a wide variety of pathways out of poverty. I've seen them improve their communities and lift up others.

I also strongly feel that the United States must reform its drug laws, which have led to lengthy incarcerations for nonviolent drug offenders that have primarily benefited the prison industrial complex—not our society as a whole. These offenders too often receive felony convictions that hinder them from working, voting, and raising capital.

I propose a two-prong prison revolution:

1. Bring entrepreneurship education to our prisons and low-income neighborhoods.

Many young men imprisoned under the drug war are would-be entrepreneurs trying to make money as small-business people. They are selling illegal products like crack cocaine and heroin, but they are indeed selling! They understand their markets, manage and organize their operations, and display other entrepreneurial traits. I can testify that entrepreneurship comes naturally to many low-income youth. They are looking for business opportunities to make money and behave entrepreneurially. Unfortunately, what they find on the streets are opportunities to sell drugs.

These young men and women are eager to participate in our economy as entrepreneurs and owners. They are desperate for knowledge of small business. Let's provide it for them!

2. Seriously consider decriminalizing nonviolent drug offenses.

The traditional labor market is often closed to individuals with criminal histories. A lack of training in skills necessary to succeed in the new economy—and employer bias stemming from a perceived liability of hiring personnel with criminal records—makes it close to impossible for people with criminal records to gain financial mobility. Those who are white get hired only half the time, and blacks only get hired 30 percent of the time. Once at the job, they can expect a 40 percent lower salary than their peers who haven't served time. The war on drugs has created a generation of disenfranchised young people saddled with lengthy prison sentences and felony records. The National Institute of Justice has found that up to 60 percent of formerly incarcerated people are not employed one year after being released.

If my proposal sounds revolutionary, consider this question: Have the benefits of the drug war—which has cost the U.S. government over a trillion dollars since President Nixon initiated it—outweighed the damage it has done?

ESCALATING INCARCERATION

The United States currently has the highest rate of incarceration in the world—higher than Russia, China, and Iran. In 1972, fewer than 350,000 people were being held in prisons and jails nationwide, compared to over 2 million today. Currently, over 7 million adults in the United States are either incarcerated, in jail, or on probation or parole. As of 2014, 1 of every 108 adults—roughly 2.3 million—were incarcerated. Blacks and Hispanics make up 1.4 million of this number. Around 2.7 million American children have parents "in the system"—in prison or on parole.

Upon release, an inmate is typically given around forty dollars and a bus ticket to the city where he or she was arrested. It's not surprising that 70 percent of people released from prison are locked up again within two years.

In her 2012 book, *The New Jim Crow: Mass Incarceration in the Age of Colorblindness*, author and legal scholar Michelle Alexander illustrated the shocking scope of mass incarceration in the United States resulting from the war on drugs—and the disproportionate and devastating impact this has had on low-income people, particularly on African American males.

No other country in the world imprisons so many of its racial or ethnic minorities. The United States incarcerates a larger percentage of its black population than South Africa did at the height of apartheid.

These stark racial disparities cannot be explained by rates of drug crime. Studies show that people of all colors use and sell illegal drugs at remarkably similar rates. If anything, whites, particularly white youth, are more likely to engage in drug crime than people of color. This is not what one would guess when entering our nation's prisons and jails, which are overflowing with ethnic minorities.

In some states, black men have been sent to prison on drug charges at rates twenty to fifty times greater than those of white men with similar charges. Former inmates will be discriminated against legally for the rest of their lives—legally denied employment, housing, education, and public benefits. This, Alexander argued, is the new Jim Crow.

In many inner cities, 80 percent of young men have prison records. These convictions will remain on their records permanently, limiting their voting rights and their ability to find employment. Currently, in all but two states, citizens with felony convictions are permanently or temporarily prohibited from voting. The United States is the only country that permits permanent disenfranchisement of felons even after completion of their sentences.

The war on drugs is also hitting poor whites, with draconian mandatory sentencing laws enacted in response to epidemic methamphetamine use and sales. The brilliant 2012 documentary *The House I Live In*, directed by Eugene Jarecki, profiles Kevin Ott, a white man from Oklahoma serving life without parole for possession of small amounts of meth due to the three-strikes law.

Who Profits from Our Prisons?

Thirty years into the drug war, over seven million people have been arrested, are on parole, or are in prison. Many have been permanently disenfranchised as a result of nonviolent drug convictions—unable to get decent jobs, vote, or travel overseas. Meanwhile, seven hundred thousand prison guards and counselors make their living off the institutions that imprison these men and women.

In his film *The House I Live In*, Jarecki made a convincing case that the war on drugs is really about fat government contracts and who gets them. State and federal spending on corrections has increased by 305 percent to $52 billion during the last two decades. On the state level, corrections is now is the second-fastest-growing budget area—behind Medicaid.

For the prison industrial complex, Jarecki noted, the war on drugs has been a huge success. For police departments who use it to get more funding and politicians who tout it to get elected, the war on drugs has also been very beneficial.

Jarecki told *Observer* editor John Mulholland in a video interview, "The tail is wagging the dog. You see this across American industries that have disproportionate and unwarranted control over the areas of policy that affect them, and so the prison industrial system in America ends up in many ways writing the laws that fill its beds."

DISCRIMINATION AGAINST FELONS

As Michelle Alexander noted in *The New Jim Crow*:

> Today it is perfectly legal to discriminate against people with criminal histories in nearly all the ways that it was once legal to discriminate against African Americans. Once you're labeled a felon, the old forms of discrimination—employment discrimination, housing discrimination, denial of the right to vote, denial of educational opportunity, denial of food stamps and other public benefits, and exclusion from jury service—are suddenly legal. As a convicted felon, you have scarcely more rights, and arguably less respect, than a black man living in Alabama at the height of

Jim Crow. We have not ended racial caste in America; we have merely redesigned it.

A felony is a life sentence in this country—regardless of the time served. Our prisons provide punishment, not rehabilitation. The result is a revolving door to prison and a legacy of poverty, dependency, violence, and incarceration that is passed down through generations.

Roughly one hundred thousand juveniles leave correctional facilities, state prison, or federal prison each year. These juveniles have a recidivism rate of 55 to 75 percent.

Letters from Prison

I first began volunteering in prisons in 1993 after one of my students was arrested for dealing small amounts of marijuana. While awaiting sentencing at Riker's Island, he was hit over the head with a chair by another inmate and died. After this tragedy I spent over three hundred hours instructing in a program run by John Jay College at Riker's Island and another two hundred hours at the Ogden Youth Home in Newark.

In 1999 I received a letter from Joe Robinson, president of the Association for Community Teamwork (ACT), an inmate-operated organization at Green Haven Correctional Facility in Dutchess County, New York. He wanted me to come teach incarcerated men about financial literacy and entrepreneurship.

Joe's poignant letter explained that he had been imprisoned since age twenty-one for killing another young man who had threatened Joe and accused him of being an accessory to an attempted robbery. In a barroom fight Joe had wrestled a gun from his would-be murderer and shot him in self-defense. Joe was sentenced to twenty-five years to life. Joe's mother had died when he was fifteen from her addiction to crack cocaine, and Joe's father had not been in his life. Forced to find his own way, he made a series of bad choices that had led him to prison.

Inside, Joe began a long journey of deep reflection that evolved into self-discovery. He became fascinated by entrepreneurship and began reading everything he could get his hands on about personal finance and business. Joe explained in his letter that he had traded cigarettes to build his library of business books. In 1995 Joe began formally teaching personal finance classes to fellow inmates.

Coincidentally, in 1993 NFTE had donated one thousand copies of my book *The Young Entrepreneur's Guide to Starting and Running a Business* to the New York Department of Corrections. This simple act sparked a twenty-year correspondence between NFTE and incarcerated people throughout the country.

At first, the letters came intermittently, one or two every week. Now the letters come almost *every day*. Since 1993 we have received over ten thousand letters from prisoners. These letters are more than just requests for more books on entrepreneurship or notes of thanks. They express a hopefulness inspired by discovering entrepreneurship and offer us a rare chance to hear directly from people whose lives have been stunted by incarceration.

The letters confirm what we already suspected about the pathway to prison—lives of poverty, little to no exposure to financial literacy, drug-related crimes, and unstable home environments. As an educator and advocate for at-risk youth, I was particularly struck in these letters by the many expressions of discouragement with the public education system.

One young man spoke about losing interest in education, gaining a full-time job, and still struggling to make ends meet. He "fell into the streets," dealing drugs and robbing to make money, "losing faith," and eventually dropping out. "My mind wasn't focused on school," he wrote. "It was concentrated on the streets. I went to school by day and sold drugs and robbed, or did whatever to make money after school."

Many letters were from former self-employed drug dealers, but not a single individual realized that drug dealing is, in fact, a business and that they had been entrepreneurs, albeit illegal ones. Once exposed to entrepreneurship, however, many prisoners showed within the pages of their letters an immense will to learn, as well as a new awareness of their own potential. One individual wrote that entrepreneurship had ignited a "flame" inside of him, giving him the ability to realize that he could start a business. Another wrote, "I am a born entrepreneur, Mr. Mariotti, and this is just the beginning of what I aspire to do."

Inmates Teaching Entrpreneurship and Mentoring (ITEM)

I was inspired by these letters to cofound Inmates Teaching Entrepreneurship and Mentoring (ITEM) with Joe Robinson in 2004. ITEM teaches inmates basic financial literacy, including how to start and run their own businesses. Joe's genius was to add a critical new component: ITEM encourages inmates to share what they're learning with their children and involve them directly in coming up with a business idea and competing in our annual business plan competitions. These imprisoned parents become involved directly in educating their own children about business and helping them find pathways out of poverty, instead of into prison.

As I crossed the bridge into Manhattan after attending one of ITEM's business plan competitions, I thought of what one prisoner had said to me as we were leaving: "This program gives us faith." Imagine how many lives would improve if this program could be replicated throughout our prison system.

In 2005 Joe married Sheila Rule, a foreign correspondent for the *New York Times*, after corresponding with her for over a year. Together, they founded the Think Outside the Cell Foundation to help the incarcerated and their families through literacy, education, and personal development. The foundation is running a national campaign to help dismantle the oppressive web of legal barriers to employment, education, voting, and more that prisoners face upon release, which make recidivism more likely. As Sheila notes on the foundation website, "When the barriers are removed, those who live in the long shadow of prison can create their own opportunities."

The foundation has also published several anthologies of writings by prisoners. In 2007 Joe published *Think outside the Cell: An Entrepreneur's Guide for the Incarcerated and Formerly Incarcerated*. He is currently writing a memoir about the effects of crack addiction on his mother and family.

Prison Entrepreneurship and Defy Ventures

Two other great programs bringing entrepreneurship education to prisoners are the Prison Entrepreneurship Program (PEP) and Defy Ventures. PEP is based on the idea that prison inmates—especially former gang leaders and drug dealers—have a massive reservoir of untapped potential. PEP seeks to redirect these men into legitimate enterprises, leveraging their street-tested entrepreneurial skill sets in the legal world.

Former Wall Street professional Catherine Rohr founded PEP in 2004 after she toured a prison and noticed that executives and inmates had more in common than one might think. Even the most unsophisticated drug dealers understand competition, profitability, risk management, and proprietary sales channels. To be successful they must be able to manage and motivate employees and build a loyal organization.

Catherine moved to Texas to start a behind-bars business plan competition. She focused on former gang leaders, drug dealers, and hustlers, linking them with top business and academic talent through an MBA-level curriculum and mentor relationships. Catherine grew PEP into a $2.5 million organization that graduated six hundred students, helped launch sixty start-ups, achieved an employment rate of 98 percent, and resulted in a return-to-prison rate of less than 5 percent. PEP attracted a network of seventy-five hundred executive volunteers and supporters (including thirty-two MBA program partners) and received national recognition and awards.

In addition to a rigorous in-prison business program, PEP teaches what it calls its "overachieving underdogs" essential life skills like moral decision making, the importance of spiritual discipline, and what employers look for when hiring.

Since studies show that former inmates are most vulnerable to recidivism within the first seventy-two hours following release, PEP provides its graduates with solutions that include housing, professional clothing for job interviews, parole mediation, transportation, and more. Graduates become part of the "free world" brotherhood network of PEP alumni and can turn to them for support, mentoring, and encouragement.

Prison Entrepreneurship Program Gets Results

In late 2013 a team of independent researchers from Baylor University led by Byron Johnson reported the following results:

- PEP outperformed all nine of the other major prison rehabilitation services in Texas. In some cases, PEP delivered a 70 to 80 percent improvement in recidivism over other models.
- The study compared ninety-four PEP graduates to a control group of more than fifty inmates who had been selected for PEP but did not participate in PEP's programs (i.e., they paroled before class began). The recidivism rate of the control group was almost identical to the state average and three to four times that of PEP's graduates.
- The researchers estimated that every dollar donated to PEP yields a 340 percent return on investment due to avoided incarceration, increased child support payments, and reduced reliance on government assistance.

Defy ventures: Transforming Dealers and Gang Leaders into Entrepreneurs

After moving on from PEP in 2009, Catherine Rohr returned to New York City and founded Defy Ventures in 2010. Defy selects paroled felons, particularly those with a history of leadership in gangs and drug rings, and puts them through a rigorous application process. Those chosen receive in-depth entrepreneurship training.

In January 2012, Defy Ventures launched its pilot group of entrepreneurs-in-training (EITs). To date, Defy EITs have launched forty-four businesses and created thirty-four employment opportunities for Defy program participants and others. Defy Ventures offers its EITs a legitimate chance to succeed as income earners, entrepreneurs, parents, and role models in their communities.

Defy's signature program engages EITs in *Shark Tank*–style business plan competitions judged by business leaders who award seed capital to winning ventures. Defy also helps incubate and finance graduates' start-ups with an eye toward creating businesses that employ other Defy grads.

In fall 2012 Defy opened enrollment to women. It continues to refine its program model to serve more future entrepreneurs and lay the foundation for national expansion.

Defy graduates have helped found over twenty companies to date, including dog walking, catering, and web services. "We target executives and the most accomplished former drug dealers we can find," Rohr told the *New York Times* in a 2013 profile. "They're both drawn to competitive environments."

THE DRUG TRADE

From reading letters from prisoners for eighteen years and visiting over twenty-five maximum-security prisons, it's obvious to me that the majority of young men in prison have worked in the drug industry. Because that is an illegal business, there's no way to legally enforce contracts, so compliance with business deals is enforced through violence. When a conflict arises between two men over money, one of them often kills or maims the other. What would be normal competitive issues in the legal business world are settled by blood in the drug business.

The seller who does well exaggerates the quality of his product and badmouths his competition. Soon he becomes the object of jealousy and resentment, which leads to beatings and killings. Another common issue is disputes over money around questions of inventory. When a drug dealer feels cheated by another dealer, it almost always leads to violence. Lost or stolen drugs also lead to conflict and killings. As a business, it is hell on earth.

Then why do young men go into the drug industry? Foremost is a lack of vision. Often these individuals do not see themselves as having a life worth living, so they jeopardize it for quick money. Most have lost interest in school or come from broken families. Many are in the foster care system. Their role models are older men who sell drugs and appear wealthy, successful, and self-employed. These drug-dealing entrepreneurs become their role models. Essentially, the drug industry provides these disenfranchised young men with a sense of family and belonging. It offers them a way to enter into business and make money.

COMMUNITIES BECOME DRUG-MONEY DEPENDENT

One of the most insidious aspects of the drug industry is that its excess profits are invested in human capital. Hundreds of thousands of young men are drawn into underground business networks that lead them to incarceration or death.

In addition, once a family's source of money from the drug industry is killed or arrested, the people dependent on that income look for someone else to supply the money. This tragic scenario helps to sustain the industry. The new head of the household will have to start dealing drugs to keep up the family income.

We must find ways to intervene and prevent these tragedies from even occurring. Any overall strategy must start with keeping kids engaged in school by structuring the curriculum around topics they want to learn about—such as entrepreneurship and making money, sales and marketing, inventions and business organization.

What about Decriminalizing Drug Addiction?

Perhaps it is also time to redefine drug addiction as a health issue and treat it like an illness, thereby eliminating the destruction of hundreds of thousands of young lives behind bars. I believe that the United States needs to take a serious look at whether we should decriminalize nonviolent drug offenses—particularly by drug users—and provide treatment instead of incarceration.

I grew up in Flint, Michigan, just one American city that has been flooded with crack cocaine and drug-dealing gangs. Flint's problems are complex, but they stem in part from rising gas prices during the 1970s OPEC oil embargo, which caused many Americans to rethink purchases of big cars from Ford, Chrysler, and Flint's largest employer, General Motors (GM).

Flint's economy was hugely dependent on GM, which by 1978 employed eighty thousand citizens in its plants. As documented in Michael Moore's 1989 film *Roger & Me*, when General Motors CEO Roger Smith closed plants in Flint and relocated them to Mexico, the impact on Flint was devastating. By 2010, only eight thousand Flint residents still had jobs at General Motors.

I have no problem with a CEO doing what he thinks is in the best interest of his shareholders—although history has not been kind to Smith, whose tenure at GM is widely viewed as a failure. But Flint has yet to recover from its addiction to a corporate giant. The city's violent crime rate skyrocketed after GM left, as entrepreneurial drug-dealing gangs filled the unemployment gap.

Unfortunately for the young men who flooded the streets of

Flint dealing crack instead of working factory jobs, and unfortunately for crack users, President Reagan signed war-on-drugs legislation in the 1980s that set the penalties for possession of crack cocaine one hundred times higher than for possession of powder cocaine, including a minimum mandatory five-year sentence for crack possession.

With an unemployment rate of 16 percent, Flint consistently makes the top of the list of the most dangerous cities in America. In 2012, twenty-seven hundred violent crimes (including sixty-six murders) were committed in this town of one hundred thousand people. Yet I can attest that Flint used to be a great place to grow up.

Today my hometown is practically a war zone, rife with gang violence, drug addiction, human trafficking, and a sick economy. For Flint's children, this situation is a catastrophe.

The response to these tragedies from Flint police officials and politicians has been a predictable call for more state and federal funds for their local war on drugs.

Fair Sentencing and Treatment

In August 2010 President Obama signed the Fair Sentencing Act, which eliminated the mandatory five-year minimum prison sentence for possession of crack cocaine and reduced the Reagan-era powder-to-crack weight ratio for sentencing from 100-to-1 to 18-to-1. This is a step in the right direction, but decriminalization and drug treatment could do more to save our cities.

Meanwhile, in Portugal the world has its first decriminalization test case—and the results, according to *Business Insider*, are "staggering." In 1999 Portugal decriminalized possession of small quantities of drugs, replacing imprisonment with treatment. Drugs like heroin, marijuana, and cocaine are still illegal in Portugal, but small-quantity infractions are settled in a special court where legal experts, psychologists, and social workers evaluate each defendant and recommend treatment or other action. Drug manufacturers and dealers are still pursued and prosecuted, but possessing small quantities is treated as a health issue.

In 2012 the *Economist* opined that "drug decriminalization has been a success everywhere it has been implemented," and urged President Obama to seriously consider it for the United States.

"Unfortunately," *the Economist* warned, "America's massive investments over the past 40 years in building up the machinery of the war on drugs have created powerful constituencies that have so far been effective in sabotaging moves in this direction."

Meanwhile, our smart, savvy urban youth know that it's tough to get a job and that they can make more money selling drugs than working a minimum-wage job anyway—and most of them have never been taught anything about legal entrepreneurship. If the only person in your young life able and willing to teach you how to set up a lucrative small business is a drug dealer, you would probably listen to him, too.

Here's the truth about the war on drugs: Because drug deals are illegal, relatively normal business disagreements over quantity, quality, or price are often settled by violence. Because drugs are illegal, the profit margins for dealing them are so high, and drug kingpins are able to employ our urban youth on every street corner of a desperate city like Flint.

Decriminalizing drugs and regulating their use through doctors and licensed pharmacies could eliminate much of the violence that arises over turf wars and drug deals gone wrong. Decriminalization could largely eliminate the highly profitable underground market in drugs and reduce not only murders and assaults but also nonviolent crime, such as robberies committed by desperate drug users.

A Success Story: Mikey Likes It Ice Cream

Certainly not every person in prison can be rehabilitated. But when rehabilitation works, the impact on society is profound. Michael "Mikey" Cole is one such success story. He grew up on New York's Lower East Side. Although his parents worked hard to provide for him and his sister, when his uncles introduced him to the street life Mike was easily seduced by the extra money he was able to earn. Mike eventually wound up in prison with a felony conviction for marijuana possession.

Once paroled, he discovered how difficult it was to get a job with his record. In an effort to turn his life around, he applied to Defy's entrepreneurship and transformation program. "I made a pledge," Mike says in his company bio, "not just to make a break with my old immaturity and lifestyle, but also to start making positive changes for the sake of those I had hurt as well. The program made me realize that if I could once earn money and build networks with people in a negative, life-sapping manner, I could do the same (or more) in a positive, life-enhancing way."

In 2012 he founded Mikey Likes It, an artisanal ice-cream company that produces organic, locally sourced ice cream in unexpected flavors such as Jack & Jill (crunchy peanut butter with strawberry preserves) and Southern Hospitality (pecan pie with praline pecans). In early 2013 he won Defy Ventures' Capital Call Business Plan Competition, receiving a much-needed influx of capital for his business as well as important new mentoring relationships.

Mikey learned his entrepreneurial skills on the street. But now he has redirected them toward legal entrepreneurship, and the sky is the limit. Mikey Likes It has already been approached by major retailers including Whole Foods, Cooper Square, and Red Bull Stadium. He couldn't have done it without the assistance of development programs like the Boys Club, which has helped him go to college and earn a degree in economics and business management; Defy Ventures; and Breathing Space, an educational incubator for ex-cons.

Breathing Space, located on thirty-two and a half acres in New York's Catskills, hosts Mikey Likes It Ice Cream's production facility, including three greenhouses for organic hydroponic food production. Breathing Space was founded by formerly incarcerated men who have also created the Hudson Link College program in New York State prisons and the Housing Works' Healthy Re-Entry Program.

Mike Cole transformed his life and is working to change others. With profits from his company, Mikey caters youth events free of charge and provides scholarships for local students.

What would have happened to this virtually unemployable young man if he had not discovered legal entrepreneurship? One thing is certain: Without Mikey Likes It Ice Cream, the world would not be as sweet a place.

Teaching young people how to participate in the free market should be a key goal of all schools. We must level the playing field by providing every young person with the intellectual property necessary to view themselves entrepreneurially and compete in our capitalistic system as both workers and owners.

Let's end the failed, costly war on drugs by decriminalizing possession of small quantities and treating drug addiction like the health issue it really is. Let's beat the dealers at their own game by bringing entrepreneurship education into our schools and making our young people business literate, so that they realize they have other options. Let's bring our local business leaders into the schools to network with our youth and inspire them to look beyond the dollars they could earn on the street corner. Let's give all our youth the knowledge they need to participate in our economy and, in the process, help save their lives.

Let's help our low-income entrepreneurs in prisons and marginalized neighborhoods compete and become business owners. Doing so will destroy the racial caste system once and for all and transform our nation.

CHAPTER 9

The Social Enterprise Revolution: Entrepreneurs Solving Social Problems

---

Social entrepreneurs are not content just to give a fish or
teach how to fish. They will not rest until they have
revolutionized the fishing industry.

—BILL DRAYTON, AUTHOR OF *LEADING SOCIAL
ENTREPRENEURS CHANGING THE WORLD*

ALL ENTREPRENEURS help society. They help allocate scarce
resources more efficiently. They create jobs and wealth.
They improve standards of living for all of us by competing to
provide better products and services at lower prices.

Entrepreneurs have also given away billions of dollars to help
their communities and solve social and environmental problems. There is a long, proud connection in the United States
between entrepreneurs and philanthropy. Ironically, some of
the most aggressive entrepreneurs in American history—like
Andrew Carnegie—have also been the most generous. As Carnegie famously said of wealthy people who only release their
wealth in their wills after death, "men who leave vast sums in
this way may fairly be thought men who would not have left it
at all had they been able to take it with them. The man who dies
thus rich dies disgraced."

Today, wealthy entrepreneurs like Bill Gates of Microsoft carry
on this tradition with the Giving Pledge, a campaign to encourage the wealthiest people in the world to make a commitment

to give most of their wealth to philanthropic causes. The Bill & Melinda Gates Foundation received $26 billion from Gates and his wife, Melinda, between 1994 and 2006. The couple has said they plan to give away over $60 billion in their lifetimes to tackle problems in health and education around the world.

Philanthropy is important and worthy, but what I'm very excited about is something that is akin to philanthropy—and yet very different. I'm talking about the revolutionary new wave of social enterprise sweeping the globe.

Social enterprises are businesses that deliberately choose to make improving some aspect of our world an integral part of their mission. These are not nonprofits or philanthropic foundations; these are businesses just as profit-driven and focused on success as any for-profit business.

I believe their focus on profit will only help them be more effective in improving our world because the surging field of social entrepreneurship uses free enterprise principles and the power of markets and ownership to solve social and environmental problems.

The Triple Bottom Line: Profit, People, Planet

Social enterprises make a difference by focusing on a triple bottom line: not only profit, but also people and the planet. Social entrepreneurs draw on their business acumen and unique knowledge of their markets to generate profit and help others. As Bill Drayton, the former McKinsey & Co. consultant who through his organization, Ashoka, has been a pioneer in the development of the social entrepreneurship field, notes, "There is nothing as powerful as a new idea in the hands of a first-class entrepreneur."

"Social entrepreneurs," Drayton writes in *Leading Social Entre-preneurs Changing the World*, "are individuals with innovative solutions to society's most pressing social problems. They are ambitious and persistent, tackling major social issues and offer-ing new ideas for wide-scale change. Rather than leaving societal needs to the government or business sectors, social entrepre-neurs find what is not working and solve the problem by chang-ing the system, spreading the solution, and persuading entire societies to move in different directions."

Another social enterprise pioneer was actor Paul Newman, who established Newman's Own in 1982 to produce and sell gro-cery items, such as salad dressing, orange juice, and popcorn. Newman wisely, in my opinion, made his company for-profit—ensuring that it would be run as efficiently and effectively as possible. Some $200 million in profits so far have been donated to Newman's Own Foundation. The foundation cosponsors the PEN / Newman's Own First Amendment Award, presented annually to a U.S. resident who has fought courageously, despite adversity, to safeguard the First Amendment's right to freedom of expression as it is applied to the written word. It also supports the fantastic SeriousFun Children's Network, which runs res-idential summer camps for children battling serious illnesses.

New Business Legal Structures Arise

In response to this surge of interest in social enterprise, new business legal structures have emerged such as the benefit cor-poration and the flexible-purpose corporation, which give com-panies more flexibility to pursue not only profit but also social and environmental goals.

A benefit corporation or B corp, for example, is required by law to benefit society as well as create profit for shareholders. B corps have to undergo annual audits to prove that they have a positive impact on the environment, the community, their employees, and society.

In 2012 Ben and Jerry's became the first subsidiary of a publicly traded company to become a certified B corporation. Founded in 1978, Ben and Jerry's is truly a pioneer in the socially responsible business movement in the United States. But in 2000, when Unilever acquired Ben and Jerry's, some had concerns that the folksy business might struggle to maintain its values.

Unilever, however, agreed to help Ben and Jerry's achieve B-corp status. Ben and Jerry's changed its charter to say that founders or the board can consider not only shareholder profit but also the community, employees, and social impact when making a business decision.

A flexible-purpose corporation or flex C is a class of corporation in California that is free from the corporate requirement to maximize profit as long as it is fulfilling at least one "special purpose" defined in its charter. This special purpose must create a benefit for society. Unlike a benefit corporation, a flexible-purpose corporation does not have to undergo yearly audits to prove that it is benefitting society. It is up to the shareholders to make sure that the corporation stays on course with its stated special purpose.

Applying Entrepreneurship to Huge Social Problems: Insights from Howard G. Buffett

Warren Buffett's son Howard G. Buffett is tackling the biggest world problem of all: hunger. Howard Buffett came upon his mission through his love of wildlife photography. Howie and I have been friends for many years, so I was eager to read his book *40 Chances: Finding Hope in a Hungry World.*

In it, Buffett says that as he traveled around the globe, he found himself training his camera increasingly on people as well as animals. "In so many endangered habitats," he notes, "people would be visibly poor and hungry." Photography became "a quiet muse nagging at my conscience."

Buffett discovers that close to a billion people worldwide are food insecure, meaning they live with hunger or fear of starvation, and deal with a long-term, persistent lack of food. He realizes that wherever people are hungry, environmentalism seems like a luxury. Buffett writes, "I was never going to make a significant difference in wildlife conservation if I wasn't willing to make a difference in the lives of people who were starving."

The Howard G. Buffett Foundation conducted an analysis that found that almost 90 percent of African farmers (more in some regions) are "fragile." They are farming overworked, tired soil. They use old seeds with poor productivity. Their families eat two or fewer meals a day and are chronically malnourished and vulnerable to disease. If they do have surplus to sell, they have nowhere to store it and no way to get it to a market. Starkly, Buffet concludes, "Millions of [these] farmers are starving to death right now."

A small increase in the productivity of a poor farmer's land can make the difference between whether the farmer's family eats or starves.

A passionate farmer himself, Buffett quickly grasps that teaching farmers to use topsoil conservation methods could both increase a farmer's harvest and discourage slash-and-burn farming and deforestation.

Solving Hunger with the Power of Markets and Ownership
The key is finding what Howie calls "market-based solutions with a social conscience." These must be sustainable, not dependent on constant flows of non-governmental organization (NGO) aid from overseas.

The book took me around the globe, with fascinating, colorful chapters describing how the Howard G. Buffett foundation has both stumbled and succeeded with different initiatives. Three clear lessons emerged:

1. Listen to the locals and help them devise methods to conserve soil and farm more effectively.
2. Encourage governments to provide clear land ownership titles and invest in agricultural science.
3. Connect small farmers to markets.

Buffett points out in his book that American farmers have benefited not only from the great soils in our "fertility belt" regions, but also "incredibly solid infrastructure, waterways, and access to vast information resources and research data" provided by our investment in agriculture since the 1700s. American farmers also benefited early in our nation's history from a land tenure system that enabled individual farmers to feel secure in ownership of their land and be able to use it as credit to develop their farms.

Buffett notes, "You can make the case that development of America's incredibly productive agricultural system came about in part because of our rules of private landownership." In addition, he says, "Government leaders must come to value connecting their country's agriculture to their farmers' ownership of their own land. These decisions will shape the future of hunger in these countries."

In contrast, subsistence farmers whom Buffette met in Honduras and Nicaragua lived in constant fear that their land would be taken from them and were afraid to invest in its future. He movingly describes their pride when they received land title documents, due to a program he works with called Agriculture for Nutrition and Health (A4NH). Once farmers know that their land can't be taken away, they can work with A4NH to plant fruit trees and cover crops and develop better watering and farming systems.

In 2003 Peruvian economist Hernando de Soto wrote a groundbreaking book, *The Mystery of Capital: Why Capitalism Triumphs in the West and Fails Everywhere Else*, which made just this point. De Soto noted that more than a decade after the fall of Marxism, the expected capitalist revolution had not occurred. He became convinced that the problem was "lack of well-defined property rights." The rate of deforestation is often highest in the world's hungriest countries. And when the government owns all the land, as in Ethiopia, it's very challenging to get farmers to change their methods, because the land they farm isn't theirs to nourish for future generations. Why shouldn't they focus on short-term yields and disregard the damage they are doing to the soil?

De Soto noted that poor people in underdeveloped countries have assets, but that their real property is often owned informally and thus cannot be used to generate capital. How exciting to read in *40 Chances* of initiatives to solve this problem!

Africa's New Privately Run Seed Industry

In Africa, meanwhile, vital state-run seed production facilities collapsed when countries were pressured by the World Bank to get their fiscal houses in order. In *40 Chances*, Buffett tells the story of Joe DeVries, a crop breeder he calls "a modern-day hero

. . . who has made a bigger impact on improving the food security of the people of Africa than just about anybody I know" by nurturing a private seed industry.

DeVries saw the vacuum that African farmers were facing when it came to seeds because their governments had retreated from seed research and development and the private market wasn't interested. He's at the center now of the Gates Foundation's Alliance for a Green Revolution in Africa (AGRA), giving fellowships to African agricultural scientists and research grants to fledgling seed companies.

This effort has created a private seed industry in Africa that is sustainable and locally appropriate. Millions of Africa's small farmers are getting productive seeds, helping them feed their families better through AGRA programs, which have launched homegrown private seed companies in sixteen African countries. DeVries estimates that this effort has fed twenty-five million people.

Brazil's government, Buffett notes, has "put together smart and motivated agricultural research that is paying off," adding that "leaders of countries grappling with food insecurity in some of the most difficult farming regions, such as sub-Saharan Africa, should find reason to hope in what has worked in Brazil." By introducing soil conservation and improvement methods to farmers working the dry, acidic soil of Brazil's *cerrado* region, the percentage of undernourished people in Brazil has dropped from 11 percent to 6 percent.

Are U.S. Farm Subsidies Ruining Our Soil?

The Mayans, the Aztecs, the Vikings, and other dead civilizations all depleted their soils through overfarming and deforestation. Buffett notes that this is happening in the United States right now, too. He argues that Washington "should end nearly eight decades of subsidizing crop production and instead subsidize and incentivize highly productive farming techniques that conserve limited natural resources—namely, soil and water."

Connect Hunger to Educations and Farmers to Markets

Linking hunger and education is another strategy that Buffett says "works just about everywhere in the world" because it connects farmers to markets. In *40 Chances* he describes traveling through Colombia with singer Shakira, whose foundation supports schools in her home country that feed over five thousand children. When school feeding programs are supplied by small, local farmers, it's a win-win.

The World Food Programme's Purchase for Progress (P4P) initiative helps create stable, reliable markets for small farmers' surplus output. It uses donors' money not to buy and ship staples from the developed to the developing world but rather to purchase aid locally from struggling small farmers. As Buffett points out, this is "not necessarily easier, but it is simpler and a stronger model" that connects farmers to markets.

After reading his book I had questions for Buffett, which he answered with even more insight into the power of markets and social enterprise to tackle hunger. What I find most interesting are his insights into the limitations of philanthropy alone and the harm some NGOs may be doing in the developing world.

STEVE MARIOTTI: In your book you are very honest about your opinion of philanthropic efforts to ease hunger that have not worked—as well as models that you think have been effective. If you had to name one principle to guide such efforts in the future, what would it be?

HOWARD G. BUFFETT: Albert Einstein said the definition of insanity is doing the same thing over and over again and expecting different results. We have had some modest success in the last twenty-five years reducing poverty and hunger on a percentage basis, but today there remain nearly 870 million people on this planet who are food insecure. In my view that is unacceptable. If we want to tackle a big problem like global hunger, we need big ideas and a different way of doing things.

SM: Helping small farmers become successful entrepreneurs so that more food becomes available in food-insecure regions is a theme throughout the book. Is there a role for a nation's government when it comes to farming and hunger?

HB: No country in history has developed its agricultural sector without government playing a major role and making significant investments to support that development. The United States did it 150 years ago with the Homestead Act to settle the West, the Morrill Act to create land-grant universities, and by building a transcontinental railroad, among other government-led efforts.

More recently, Brazil has spent the last few decades making huge investments in agricultural research, infrastructure, and neutralizing the soil in vast areas of the country's interior to make it available to agriculture. They made some mistakes that had negative consequences for their environment, but they are learning from those early mistakes and have course-corrected in terms of their biodiversity requirements. Now they are working to tie smallholder production to their government procurement programs to further accelerate development of the country's poorest farmers, all while building a conservation-based farming system that looks very different from ours yet competes on par with the United States in terms of corn and especially soybean production.

Many countries in Africa have populations where 60 percent to 80 percent are smallholder farmers. Governments have to play a huge role to ensure these farmers can support their own food needs but also connect to markets to generate income. The wisest role a nation's government can play is to make significant investments in research and extension. I would put a land-grant university in every country in Africa. Africa is a continent of fifty-four countries—there is no one-size-fits-all solution, and their system of agriculture, if done well, won't really look like the United States system. It will look more like Brazil, but each country needs to invest in agriculture based on the specific needs of their population and the resources available.

SM: You speak out against "monetization," the NGO practice of selling in-kind aid—such as grain shipped from the United States—locally to raise money to pay for other needs or NGO expenses. European aid programs are now providing cash aid instead, but American NGOs are lagging behind. Why? Do you expect this to change soon?

HB: Monetization is when NGOs are allowed to take excess U.S.-grown commodities that are not used for meeting emergency needs and sell those commodities into local markets for cash, which is then used to support the NGO's programs. If you think about what that means in practical terms, it means that if I'm an organization working to support and develop smallholder farmers in the developing world, I'm dumping U.S. commodities onto the very local markets I'm in theory trying to help, which means that smallholder farmers will get less for anything they grow and try to sell.

The United States is unique among donor countries in that it provides most of its food aid in the form of in-kind commodities. This has become inefficient in terms of shipping costs and timing and also means that the United States provides less food aid than it could if operating on a cash basis. It's a model that is outdated—the same amount of aid if delivered in the form of local procurement dollars would do more to meet the needs of more hungry people quicker, especially in emergency situations, while also supporting growth of local economies, which is the key to long-term food security.

SM: Instead of using donors' money to buy food and ship it to struggling regions, the World Food Programme's P4P purchases commodities for local food assistance from local smallholder farmers and encourages local governments to link food procurement for school meals to small-scale local farmers. Your foundation and the Gates Foundation both support P4P. Any new developments to report?

HB: Our foundation has had a lot of success investing in local procurement systems like P4P. Our experience has been that figuring out how to connect smallholder farmers to markets is a faster, more sustainable way to address food insecurity.

In Central America we really took it a step further by investing in building the productive capacity of smallholder farmers as well as their capacity to do business. The next phase of P4P is still to be determined—there is a lot of work to be done still to determine the key lessons learned—but we are excited that in Central America, there is a real effort under way to do what Brazil did in terms of connecting government procurement needs to smallholder farmer production, especially for school feeding programs. If a government can connect those procurement needs to investments in smallholder farmers, you can really see how that can be a more effective form of investment in a country's food security.

SM: Agriculture for Basic Needs or A4N is another initiative you supported in Central America that develops smallholder farmers by teaching them sustainable farming methods, business skills, a market focus, and financial literacy so that they can enter and thrive in the local economy. How is that going? Do you envision A4N programs spreading to other regions?

HB: We invested in A4N to test and pilot these ideas for thousands of farmers and their families across Central America. We view our philanthropy as the initial risk capital for testing new ideas. A4N was a great example of something we supported, demonstrated its effectiveness, and then worked with Catholic Relief Services (CRS) to translate what we learned into an advocacy agenda that could inform investments and efforts at scale.

Our foundation cannot fund ideas like this at scale; we don't have the resources, and even if we did, it's my belief that our funding is better utilized on the risk and innovation side, not in the scaling up of proven ideas. So in our view we accomplished what we set out to accomplish with A4N. CRS changed its approach to smallholder development as a result of this effort (and others), to focus more on value chains, not just production, and A4N is informing the governments' approach to extension in the region.

HELP PEOPLE CONNECT TO MARKETS, AND THEY WILL HELP THEMSELVES

Another social entrepreneurship harnessing the power of markets is Poonam Ahluwalia, executive director of YouthTrade and the Youth, Entrepreneurship, and Sustainability (YES) Campaign at Cambridge College in Massachusetts. She has long been a leader in efforts in igniting and sustaining entrepreneurial efforts around the world and is a passionate leader on behalf of youth worldwide.

In the late 1990s she began to work with the Education Development Center in Newton, Massachusetts, using funds from the U.S. Agency for International Development (USAID) to create workshops to promote global learning, health, and education. Feedback from workshops that she helped run in South America, Africa, and her native India led Ahluwalia to zero in on the serious global problem of youth unemployment. She founded YES to address the problem in 1998. The bottom-line goal: To create millions of new young entrepreneurs around the world to address the lack of jobs for the coming generation.

"There are not enough jobs in the private and public sectors to absorb millions of young people who are in the labor market," Ahluwalia told me, adding, "Vocational training without job creation is moot."

In 2011 Ahluwalia harnessed the power of markets to aid her mission by founding YouthTrade, which certifies young mission-driven entrepreneurs and works with them to help place their products at participating companies, such as Whole Foods Market, Nordstrom, Babson College, and Conscious Capitalism. Young entrepreneurs gain access to key retail markets.

Ahluwalia said she had big goals for YouthTrade, including building a global marketplace for the products of entrepreneurs in the program, linking with universities to promote entrepreneurial principles in their career centers, and setting up a "champions" program for corporations to buy a percentage of their supplies from YouthTrade-certified companies.

The best asset for a social entrepreneur, she says, is not knowing what she supposedly can't do:

I think my main asset is that I am ignorant and do not know much, and that allows me to go forth basically unaware that I can fail. I believe that nothing is impossible and that anyone can accomplish whatever they set their mind and heart upon. My main expertise is in community organizing and creating simple architectures where everyone can have a role. Since my childhood I have felt enraged by the inequities of life and the needless poverty in this wealthy world. My deepest desire has always been to level the playing field and work toward the possibility that everyone has an opportunity to fulfill their promise.

USING SOCIAL ENTERPRISE TO HELP CAMBODIANS

I found another very simple yet very exciting example of social enterprise on my trip to Cambodia. The Cambodian people have suffered greatly—from the French occupation, the civil war, American bombings, Vietnamese invasions, and brutal genocide at the hands of the Khmer Rouge. Nonetheless, Cambodia is booming in many ways. The people are full of energy and work hard, the cities are bustling, and positivity abounds.

On my travels I met the extraordinary social entrepreneur Janice Wilson and learned about her social enterprise, Arjuni. Janice found her way to Cambodia through an unlikely path. After initially dropping out of law school to pursue her dance career with Wynton Marsalis, she eventually returned to and graduated from Columbia after a six-year hiatus. She went to Cambodia in late 2008 to provide legal assistance during the condominium boom their economy experienced. During that time she began to notice the prevalence of women who had been involved in and abused by the sex trafficking market. Janice wanted to help, but she also had a long-held dream of wanting to start her own business.

Determined to get involved in building better lives for women who were struggling to emerge from the sex trade, she soon found a way to start a business. Her idea was simple: Help these women sell their hair instead of their bodies.

Janice traveled to villages around the Cambodian country-side to meet with women interested in getting involved. When a woman wanted to sell her hair, Janice would cut it in exchange for an amount equal to four months of salary. Now her company has several collection teams that travel the countryside. They have performed this life-changing exchange with over seven thousand women! In the past three years, the business has quadrupled.

Cambodian hair has a global reputation for its quality, and Janice's company is the leading manufacturer. Her company is now housed in a factory, where her employees fabricate, clean, and package the hair before shipping it and selling it all over the world. Because of the company's success, Janice has been able to hire forty-two women, most of whom have emerged from traumatic circumstances related to sex trafficking and domestic violence.

Young Entrepreneurs Choosing Social Enterprise

It's very exciting to see what young entrepreneurs are accomplishing in the new field of social enterprise. Carrie Rich is cofounder of the Global Good Fund, Blu2Green LLC, and Teens for Technology. From social entrepreneurship to leadership to mentorship, Carrie provides advice for those who seek to achieve their full leadership potential. She's been passionate about social entrepreneurship, leadership, and development since age fourteen, when she cofounded Teens for Technology, an organization dedicated to improving computer literacy. The organization raised $1.2 million, funded computer literacy training on one hundred thousand computers throughout Jamaica, hired a local staff that today is self-sustaining, established a school club network in Jamaica, and expanded to two countries.

In 2011 she cofounded the for-profit social business Blu2Green LLC, which produces products handmade in the United States out of recycled materials. Blu2Green employs people with special needs to repurpose medical blue wrap—waste that would otherwise rest in landfills—into accessories and clothing items.

Today, Carrie's new social enterprise, the Global Good Fund, accelerates the development of high-potential young leaders who tackle the world's social issues through entrepreneurship. The fund selects promising young leaders for a fellowship program that pairs aspiring entrepreneurs with seasoned executives who serve as coaches. The fund also helps aspiring social entrepreneurs with access to a network of investors.

As Carrie explained to me, "We provide leadership assessment resources, a network of peer leaders, content expertise, and targeted funding. We've invested in nineteen entrepreneurs to date and aim to double our investment next year. We believe that our fellows are key leverage points in our global society—that if we invest in them, we'll make the most significant, long-term impact possible."

The Current State of Social Enterprise in the United States

As a field, social enterprise is barely off the ground, which makes me even more optimistic about the revolutionary improvements that social entrepreneurs will make in our world in the future. The Great Social Enterprise Census is a new initiative seeking to measure the size and impact of social entrepreneurship in America. Although its current data is limited and far from comprehensive, it has found so far that American social enterprises qualify as small businesses on average, by both revenue and number of employees. Over 90 percent of them are focused on solving problems here at home rather than overseas.

The census found that those who have responded control over $300 million in revenue and employ an estimated fourteen thousand people in twenty-eight states. Around 40 percent of the social enterprises surveyed were found to have fewer than five employees; just 8 percent had more than one hundred. Roughly 20 percent are focused on economic development, 16 percent are focused on workforce development, 12 percent are targeting energy and the environment, 11 percent are in education, and 7 percent are working internationally.

Interestingly, the census estimated that 60 percent of U.S. social enterprises were created in 2006 or later, with 29 percent created since 2011. In addition, as InSight director Ben Thornley pointed out in his November 2012 *Huffington Post* article "The Facts on U.S. Social Enterprise," there are likely hundreds of thousands of organizations in the United States that can and should self-identify as social enterprises. He estimates that in actuality this economic sector may employ as many as 10 million people, with revenues of $500 billion or almost 3.5 percent of total U.S. GDP.

In short, social enterprise is poised to become a booming sector of the American economy. Having this census data will help us understand the potential impact of social enterprise on our nation and will encourage investors and policymakers to discover what more they can do to, as Thornley put it, "help put private enterprise to work in the service of public good."

In the United Kingdom, data indicates that roughly 7 percent of all small businesses meet the definition of social enterprise— representing sixty-eight thousand enterprises, £24 billion in revenue, and employing eight hundred thousand people. This news has motivated the United Kingdom to position itself as a social enterprise leader, with policymakers working to attract investors and create a supportive environment. The United States should do the same and recognize the potential power of social enterprise to not only tackle social problems but improve the nation's overall economic health—which in turn is good for everyone!

Some Advice for Social Entrepreneurs

If I had to do it over again today, I would organize NFTE as a for-profit social enterprise instead of a nonprofit. Regardless, the most important thing I can tell you is that if you're running a social enterprise and you attract investors, you will need to design a data collection and research strategy to show donors and peers that you're actually achieving your goals. The majority of investors in social enterprise and nonprofits are hard-nosed businesspeople, and they expect a quantifiable return on their investments. Social enterprise is just like any other business: You must prove that you are meeting your triple bottom line. It is absolutely necessary that from day one you think about how you are going to quantify and prove that you get results.

I learned this lesson the hard way. One of my early experiences was with a top philanthropist in New York City, an early supporter of my foundation, who abruptly stopped funding us. After several brush-offs, I finally managed to secure a meeting. When I asked why she had stopped her donations to NFTE, she became annoyed and asked, "Where's your research? Where are your numbers?" She shook an investment report in front of my face. "Like this! You need numbers to prove your outcomes!"

Completely rattled, I asked her what the numbers on the paper she was waving in front of me meant. "This is our investment report," she replied. "These numbers prove we're getting a return on our investment. Where are your numbers?"

You Must Quantify and Prove Your Results

I knew from my own experience how much entrepreneurship education was doing for at-risk youth, but how could I prove that to a tough, business-minded investor like her? The answer was research. Social enterprise is just like any other business: You must prove that you are meeting your triple bottom line. It is absolutely necessary that from day one you think about how you are going to quantify and prove that you get results.

After my former funder was done berating me, I asked her if she would fund the research that NFTE desperately needed, but she declined. I left feeling hopeless, wondering if perhaps I should close NFTE and seek another career.

To my surprise, the next day a fifteen-thousand-dollar check from her arrived at my office. This kind gesture wasn't enough to fund a study, but it was a start. More importantly, she had taught me a very critical lesson: It wasn't enough to gather anecdotal evidence of the positive things we were accomplishing. If we were going to ask donors to fund NFTE to the tune of thousands, even millions, of dollars, we would need statistics demonstrating that we were a worthwhile investment. Otherwise, the money would (and should!) flow to other nonprofits or social enterprises that could show they were achieving their aims.

I realized that we had to develop a theory of change for NFTE, to understand the intended outcomes of our programs, and begin collecting data on those outcomes by putting a long-term research strategy in place. I recommend that if you are running a social enterprise, you do the same.

Research: Expensive, Time-Consuming, and Worth It

Our first study, conducted with Professor Andrew Hahn from Brandeis University's Heller Graduate School and its Center for Youth and Communities, established NFTE as a leader in entrepreneurship education for at-risk youth. The pilot study had a small sample size but nonetheless showed that NFTE's work had a positive impact on the young people it served, improving both business knowledge and business formation. Interestingly, the young people's participation in volunteerism increased as well, demonstrating that they were more socially conscious. To the best of my knowledge, it was the first random assignment study done on business education. The Brandeis/NFTE partnership lasted from 1993 to 1997. It was expensive and required a lot of work, but the results were encouraging. The group of NFTE students outperformed the control group on key outcomes, including business formation rates and entrepreneurial knowledge.

We have continued to make research central to our mission

and have conducted a series of further studies, including one with the Koch Foundation in 1998 on business formation and attitudes toward business among NFTE students; a Harvard Graduate School of Education study in 2001–2002 of NFTE students in two Boston public high schools; a 2006 Brandeis University and Harvard University multisite evaluation of NFTE students; and a 2009–2010 study at a Chicago public high school. As a result of our ability to quantify and prove our results, we have become a highly replicated program.

Incorporate Ongoing Assessment

If you are working in social enterprise, I can't recommend strongly enough that you, too, incorporate ongoing assessment into your organization. To do this you must first identify the anticipated outcomes of your program. Just like the owner of a business must designate the business's unit of sale, you must choose your unit of change so that you can calculate your costs per unit and quantify your effectiveness.

Next, you must conduct research that can empirically demonstrate whether your enterprise is worthy of investment—that it is truly a force for social good. If it is not, you are wasting scarce resources, just like an entrepreneur who is failing to make a profit. That is a signal to either adjust the business or close it.

I also hope you will choose to share your findings with the public, even if they are disappointing. Even disappointing results can be valuable. Share the good and the bad.

A major discovery in the Brandeis/NFTE research, for example, was that fewer kids wanted to go into business after taking NFTE's program than before. At first I was devastated, but then I realized that it was a compliment to our curriculum—the students had learned how demanding starting a small business was!

Qualitative Data Is Real, Too

Finally, even though I just emphasized quantitative research, never forget that the voices of the people you are serving are also essential. Be sure to collect their personal stories and testimonials. Follow up with them. At NFTE we have an office dedicated to following up with our graduates for many years to see how they are doing. In my opinion, what our alumni say about us and how our lives change is the best proof we have that our programs work.

Anecdotes and stories are powerful motivators and are a form of evidence that will be valuable to your program. Focus groups and narrative surveys are powerful tools for getting at information about where your program is working and where it needs to improve. Key insights will come out of both quantitative and qualitative methodologies.

THE FUTURE LOOKS BRIGHT

With social enterprise just starting to blossom, these are very exciting times for entrepreneurs and corporate executives alike to realize that including people and the planet along with profit in a business's bottom line will always benefit the business.

Increasingly, investors are looking to, as eBay cofounder Jeff Gardner put it in his 2013 TED talk, "bet on good people doing good things."

If that's not revolutionary, I don't know what is.

CHAPTER 10

An Entrepreneur's Manifesto

C OUNTLESS TIMES over the years, when a NFTE kid was struggling to express a business idea to me, I would snap my finger two inches in front of his or her face and say, "That's what you need."

The snap represented the concise, attention-grabbing pitch needed to instantly convey the unique contribution that business idea was going to make. The snap was the business idea rigorously and ruthlessly stripped down to its essence—one sentence that would clearly communicate the business's competitive advantage to customers, investors, suppliers, and partners.

Come to one of NFTE's business pitch competitions—whether it's for middle schoolers in Washington, DC, or the top competitors from every corner of the earth in our Global Challenge—and you will hear that snap in real time. Whether it's a T-shirt business taking orders at lunchtime in the school cafeteria or the next Facebook or Google, the entrepreneur who cannot produce that snap faces a tough road to success.

THE HUMAN RACE'S COMPETITIVE ADVANTAGE

I hope this book has persuaded you that the human race's competitive advantage is entrepreneurship. Our "snap" is that we each have the ability to create something out of nothing that will benefit not just ourselves but all humankind. Unlike so many failed ideological revolutions of the past, the Entrepreneurship

Revolution cuts along the grain of human nature. It does not try to transform human beings into some new super-race but instead aims to nurture and bring forth the talents and feelings that are already there. Some of the practical concepts of business ownership may be hard for some to grasp at first, but the impulses that drive the entrepreneur are basic to the human spirit.

The Entrepreneurship Revolution sounds utopian, but it's not. In fact, it is the most practical way I know to address so many of the ills plaguing the world economy today, from underemployment and a massive skills gap to the lack of opportunity for billions of people in the rising generations around the world. It's the best way I know to address the enduring inequalities of opportunity and wealth within and between nations—not just to redistribute the world's wealth, but to create new sources of prosperity.

The Entrepreneurship Revolution is not utopian because it's based on a hard-headed calculation: If we can cut the rate of new business failure by even 1 to 2 percent, we put ourselves on a glide path to eliminate poverty within the next two generations.

I have seen the Entrepreneurship Revolution's principles play out in my own life. In my hometown of Flint, Michigan, a once-thriving community was ravaged by economic complacency, overdependence on a single behemoth employer, and failure to nourish its original entrepreneurial spirit. In my classrooms in some of the roughest neighborhoods of New York City I have seen my students' lives transformed by the empowering idea of entrepreneurship. In remote villages in Cambodia I have seen the entrepreneurial flame miraculously kept alive in the face of some of the greatest horrors of the twentieth century.

As I've explored in this book, we're living in a new and golden age for entrepreneurial scholarship, with more research being done now on what makes a business owner tick, what conditions promote the growth of new enterprises, and what legal, financial, and cultural conditions encourage entrepreneurship. We are benefitting from the insights of great thinkers ranging from Friedrich Hayek and Ludwig von Mises to Cathy Ashmore and Angela Duckworth. Their efforts have greatly enriched the field of entrepreneurial scholarship.

A Crossroads for the Free-Market Model

Nonetheless, the world is at a crossroads. Pockets of entrepreneurial energy and innovation are popping up that are as vital and productive as any in history. Entire regions of the globe are swept up in the market revolution, emerging from a long-misguided age of state control. In countries rich and poor, surveys show, the entrepreneur is an increasingly respected and admired figure, recognized as the adrenaline jolt the global economy needs to advance to a new state of prosperity.

But the financial crisis that began in 2008 has also raised new questions about the free-market model. The creative destruction that Schumpeter first identified has proven particularly disruptive to established business interests in the Internet Age. Not just individual jobs but entire professions—travel agents, printers, journalists—have been eradicated or challenged by the Internet. Governments around the world stepped in to prop up failing businesses, in the process running up debts that future generations will have to pay somehow. The free-market capitalist model that seemed to have triumphed with the collapse of the Soviet Union is being questioned once more, in Washington and London no less than in Beijing or Mumbai.

ENTREPRENEURSHIP CAN AND MUST BE TAUGHT

The Entrepreneurship Revolution is by no means won. We have to redouble our efforts and reclaim ground we thought we had secured. As I have argued here, the first battle must be fought in our schools, where my dream is that entrepreneurial education will one day be as much a part of the standard curriculum as reading and math. We don't have time anymore for pointless arguments over whether entrepreneurship can be taught. The only questions for us now are whether entrepreneurship is taught well or poorly, and whether we have the will to do it.

The idea of the entrepreneurial mind-set is, I believe, critical to the effective teaching of entrepreneurship. The good news: That mind-set isn't some special gift for the chosen few but is part of the mental makeup of every person on the planet. It does not have to be created, only cultivated.

Entrepreneurship teachers are the foot soldiers of this revolution, the unsung heroes who deserve far more support and resources than they have been given to date. We have learned that the best entrepreneurship teachers should be grounded in both real and theoretical knowledge. We also now have a better understanding of the role that government can—and cannot—play in promoting an entrepreneurial economy and cultivating an entrepreneurial mind-set. Statist attempts to remake economies from the top down have been exposed by the history of the past one hundred years as invariably leading to totalitarian nightmares. What economist Peter Klein has said bears repeating: "What entrepreneurs need is secure property rights, the rule of law, and sound money. The best thing government can do for entrepreneurs is get out of their way."

Today, Everyone Is an Investor

In the fields of technology and finance, the Entrepreneurship Revolution is already in full swing, with no one yet able to say how far it will take us. Already the power of the Internet to crowdsource ideas and funding has transformed the age-old financing struggle that every new business owner faces.

The Web has undercut the need to find a single big financial angel to get a business going. Now an entire entrepreneurial project can be funded with far smaller slices of capital assembled from thousands of individual investors. With just a few keystrokes, entrepreneurs from Boston to Bangladesh can now access critical market research, once a carefully guarded secret in the hands of a lucky few.

I see constantly with my own students how the Web has opened up not just new business niches in existing industries but whole new industries that no one had considered. There were no webpage design consultants, no content curators, no cybersecurity analysts when I started teaching in the early 1980s.

It would be foolish to try to predict where the Digital Revolution will take us in the coming decades, but for entrepreneurs the trend is clear: toward more power, more autonomy, and more knowledge about themselves and the marketplace.

Happiness Is Revolutionary, Too

There is one more benefit of the global Entrepreneurship Revolution that we have yet to explore in depth: It has the power to make us happy.

Economists have traditionally avoided tackling "happiness" as a concept. Tastes differ. Times change. What makes one person happy may bore another to distraction. Happiness carries with it moral judgments best left to theologians and life coaches. To avoid even discussing the topic, nineteenth-century economists invented their own value-neutral concept of "utility," a quality that one seeks to "maximize" along an "indifference curve." (No wonder economics is called the "dismal science.") Utility, the great English economist Alfred Marshall wrote in his 1890 classic, *Principles of Economics*, is the profession's "correlative to Desire or Want." Marshall explained that desires "cannot be measured directly, but only indirectly, by the outward phenomena to which they give rise: and that in those cases with which economics is chiefly concerned the measure is found in the price which a person is willing to pay for the fulfillment or satisfaction of his desire."

In recent years, however, a new science of happiness has arisen to fill the void that Marshall and his economist peers created. The Himalayan kingdom of Bhutan was widely mocked when it introduced a "gross national happiness" measure in 1972, but now other countries are exploring at least a variation on the idea. There is a clear recognition that traditional measures such as GDP growth or per-capita income do not capture the sum total of what makes a person feel fulfilled in life. And it turns out, according to multiple studies, that some of the happiest people on Earth are entrepreneurs.

WHY ARE ENTREPRENEURS SO HAPPY?

That entrepreneurs are happier than others might seem surprising, given the well-noted anxieties that come with starting a business. Even in the brave new world I see developing for entrepreneurs, many will fail at their first ventures. Entrepreneurs routinely say that theirs is a 24/7/365 profession, one in which you are never really off the clock. There are always bills coming due, regulations to obey, employees to motivate, competitors to be watched, and customers to be wooed. There is always the yawning prospect of failure, often of a very personal yet very public nature. Entrepreneurs are their own bosses, and there is always the promise of a big payoff someday, but the journey is typically difficult and stress-inducing.

Yet when Ethan Mollick and Matthew Bidwell, two management professors at the Wharton School of Business, polled some eleven thousand graduates of their prestigious school on their satisfaction with their career and work-life balance, two conclusions stood out: People with more money were on average happier than people with less, and Wharton grads who went on to become entrepreneurs scored unexpectedly high on the life satisfaction scale.

In every field that the two studied, including technology, finance, and consulting, the Wharton MBAs who struck out on their own reported higher levels of job and life satisfaction—happiness—than their peers, even if they were not earning more money.

"We were surprised that entrepreneurship was such a dominant factor," Mollik told TheStreet.com in a 2013 interview. "Entrepreneurs are working really hard," Mollik explained, "but there's a sense that they have control over their own time, even if they're putting in a huge number of hours."

It's not just Wharton grads or only American entrepreneurs who express happiness with their career choice. In a study of data collected over ten years, economists Alex Coad of the University of Sussex and Martin Binder of the University of Kassel in Germany concluded that the self-employed in the United Kingdom experience significantly higher "life satisfaction" than wage earners, especially if they are entrepreneurs by choice and not by necessity. In their 2014 paper "How Satisfied Are the Self-Employed?" they wrote, "In our analysis, we found that individuals moving from regular employment into self-employment . . . experience a positive and significant increase in life satisfaction, that actually increases from the first year of self-employment to the second." The findings hold even though the earnings of British entrepreneurs on average are lower than those of salaried persons.

Autonomy, whether in business or life, seems directly correlated with elevated levels of happiness. Researchers looking at results from the 2014 Gallup-Healthways Well-Being Index found that entrepreneurship makes the day go faster, and that entrepreneurs are more eager to expand their horizons. The product of more than 273,000 surveys, the Gallup research found that entrepreneurs tend to report more positive experiences in an average workday. They were also more likely to report having learned something new in the most recent day at the office, even while they reported slightly higher levels of stress.

"The same intellectual curiosity and energy needed to start and run a business may also drive entrepreneurs to seek out and take advantage of opportunities to learn or do something interesting or exciting on a regular basis," reported Gallup researchers Dan Witters, Sangeeta Agrawal, and Alyssa Brown. They noted that "entrepreneurs also have creative strategic control of their business and manage their own schedule to execute their business plan. Thus, they may have more flexibility to pursue interesting and exciting learning opportunities and activities than other workers."

The Global Entrpreneurship Monitor Explores Entrepreneurship and Well-Being

This trend has become so noticeable that in 2013 the Global Entrepreneurship Monitor (GEM)—the gold standard for international research on entrepreneurship trends and scholarship—reported the results of a major study it had conducted into the relationship between entrepreneurship and personal feelings of well-being. The GEM research largely confirmed the image of the happy entrepreneur, albeit with a few nuances.

That the GEM brain trust thought happiness was a study-worthy topic is itself of interest. As you've read earlier in this book, GEM researchers have produced groundbreaking work on virtually every aspect of the entrepreneurial experience—from the role of immigrants in business formation to cross-national comparisons regarding fear of business failure and social standing among entrepreneurs worldwide. But only recently did the GEM researchers try to measure what might be termed the sheer joy of starting and running a business. The results were so positive that in its 2013 Global Report, GEM stated simply that "entrepreneurs are among the happiest people in the world."

The study, which polled nearly two hundred thousand people in seventy countries, asked respondents to measure their subjective "well-being" based on their agreement or disagreement with a series of statements such as, "The conditions of my life are excellent," and "So far, I have obtained the important things I want in life."

"Our idea," explained José Ernesto Amorós, one of the report's coauthors, "is to contribute to a better understanding about what influences a population's perceptions about well-being and how that consequently shapes entrepreneurship indicators."

The GEM study proves that entrepreneurs are a particularly contented lot, happier with their lives than the general population, especially if they are business owners by choice and not by necessity. The longer they stayed in an entrepreneurial venture, the researchers found, the happier they became.

Entrepreneurship More Rewarding for Women?

According to GEM, entrepreneurship proves particularly rewarding for women. Amorós notes one interesting finding, that "female entrepreneurs in innovation-driven economies exhibit on average a higher degree of subjective well-being than males. This initial assessment opens up possibilities for exploring the role of women and men entrepreneurs beyond the traditional notion of development generally associated with economic indicators."

There were differing levels of reported well-being between regions and across income lines, but the bottom-line findings from GEM were remarkably consistent with the results for the Wharton MBAs, British business owners, and the Gallup poll-takers. All other things equal, starting and running your own business makes you a happier person.

Entrepreneurs May Achieve Better Life-Work Balance

Surprisingly, the GEM survey found that, particularly in the developed world, entrepreneurs even report a more satisfactory "life-work balance" than their nonentrepreneurial peers. Because of the compelling evidence that entrepreneurs are happier, the report recommended that "education and training related to entrepreneurship should perhaps pay more attention to these 'softer' aspects that may get limited attention but could play an important role for entrepreneurs."

Nolan Bushnell, the founder of Atari, Pong, and Chuck E.

Cheese's, is one of the great entrepreneurs of the last fifty years. He recently told me, "No matter how bad the bad times are, they are really much better than being in a cubicle working for 'The Man.' The most important thing you have is your family and seeding the next generation. I learned about entrepreneurship from my dad and have been in the field for sixty years."

Kelso's Capitalist Manifesto

I spoke earlier in this book of my admiration for entrepreneur and business giant Louis Kelso. In 1958, when the United States was embarking on a surge in wealth and prosperity unprecedented in world history, he and coauthor Mortimer Adler published *The Capitalist Manifesto*, a defense of capitalism explicitly modeled after another famous manifesto written by Karl Marx and Friedrich Engels just over a century earlier. The timing of Kelso and Adler's book may seem odd to us today, but even then they saw challenges to the capitalist ideal and a creeping belief that a maximally free market was not something worth defending. "*The Capitalist Manifesto,*" they wrote, "is intended to replace *The Communist Manifesto* as a call to action, first of all in our own country, and then, with our country's leadership, everywhere else in the world. It is our industrial power and capital wealth, together with our institutions of political liberty and to establish economic liberty and justice for all."

I titled this book *An Entrepreneur's Manifesto* because I hope it will be a call to action every bit as vital and relevant to our times as their book was to the mid-twentieth century. A manifesto, by definition, is a rallying cry, a recruitment pitch, a sermon, and a warning all rolled into one. I'm optimistic that the world can embark on a new age of prosperity and innovation if we tap the true power of entrepreneurship. I am less certain that we will usher this great new revolution if we do not protect, nurture, and encourage free markets, entrepreneurship, and entrepreneurship education around the world.

THE ENTREPRENEUR'S BILL OF RIGHTS

To that end, I am proposing an Entrepreneur's Bill of Rights, modeled on the great amendments to our Constitution that have helped preserve and extend liberty and prosperity to more and more sectors of our society over the past 250 years.

Specifically, I believe that every entrepreneur in every industry, class, and country should enjoy the following:

1. The Right to Create

This may seem a freedom we can take for granted, but there remain too many barriers to entrepreneurship in the United States and around the world. Some barriers are legal, such as red tape or excessive, complicated taxation, but many are mental. My very first NFTE kids had no idea that entrepreneurship was an option. They didn't know that they had an alternative to a future of low-end, low-paying work in an unwelcoming job market. I have argued here that entrepreneurship and entrepreneurial principles should be an integral part of the curriculum starting at the pre-K level. The consistent message of those lessons should always be that everyone has the right and the unique talent to create something new and bring it into the world.

2. The Right to Destroy

Every new business has the potential to destroy another person's livelihood—and that's OK. Even a new corner deli makes its mark, disrupting the status quo, and challenging those already in the market to get better or move aside. Schumpeter's "creative destruction" is a core concept of entrepreneurship, one that has long guided my own thinking about how economies should work and how business should be regulated. Yet one could hardly blame a young entrepreneur in 2014 for fearing that his right to destroy—to offer a service or product that upsets the existing balance of market forces—is under attack. During the global financial crisis, banks that made bad loans were bailed out, car companies that failed to adjust to changing tastes and foreign competition received taxpayer dollars to stay in business. While entrepreneurial start-ups struggle (on their own) to get a foot in the door, giant competitors have a seat at the table when regulations are drawn up or laws are passed. If the entrepreneur has a better idea than the established interests, he or she should be able to take them on. And it should be a fair fight.

3. The Right to Fail

Of course we want to help the next generations of entrepreneurs work smarter and faster and become better at job creation. This is the best way to crush poverty and raise global living standards. But success can't happen without failure. Some of the world's greatest fortunes were built by entrepreneurs working on their fifth or sixth try. Failure is OK and in some cases should even be celebrated. A nation with too few commercial bankruptcies is suffering from a lack of dynamism.

In his important 2009 book *Meltdown: A Free-Market Look at Why the Stock Market Collapsed, the Economy Tanked, and Government Bailouts Will Make Things Worse*, Thomas E. Woods Jr., a senior fellow at the Ludwig von Mises Institute, provided a devastating analysis of how America's refusal to honor the "right to fail" undermined the housing market, crashed the stock market, tanked the economy, and ran up bills that will take decades to pay off. While stores were being shuttered on Main Streets across the country (and the world), the biggest players on Wall Street were deemed "too big to fail." Unfortunately, as Woods explained, "The longer they are kept on life support, the more they drain capital and resources away from fundamentally sound firms that could put those resources to much more productive use from the consumers' point of view. Keeping such firms alive via government bailouts discourages rather than encourages capital formation and economic recovery."

4. The Right to a Simple, Fair Tax Code

To tax is to choose. If we want to see the coming Entrepreneurship Revolution succeed, governments must get the incentive structures in their tax codes right. Favoring existing business in the tax codes or placing undue burdens on job creators and small entrepreneurs can have disastrous effects. "Tax and regulation are key levers for improving a country's business environment," according to the 2013 Ernst & Young G20 Entrepreneurship Barometer. "Countries that offer favorable tax rates, simplify procedures, and provide entrepreneurial support will more likely enjoy high numbers of start-ups. In turn, these ventures become significant creators of jobs and tax revenue as they progress up the growth curve." Worryingly, the United States currently ranks thirteenth out of twenty in the Ernst & Young tax and regulation survey, trailing Saudi Arabia, Japan, and Russia.

5. The Right to Collaborate

The entrepreneur is stereotyped as a loner, an obsessive who cares only for the next big chance. In reality, the opposite is true. An entrepreneur must be a social creature. You can't understand the market if you don't understand the billions of potential customers who constitute it. In any start-up business that grows beyond the founder, the entrepreneur must also be a manager and a mentor. Thomas Edison, often portrayed as the classic lone genius, was in fact a world-class collaborator who managed a vast team of innovators and created some of the largest commercial organizations in the country.

6. The Right to Seek New Opportunity

The winners of the Entrepreneurship Revolution will be those nations most welcoming to people with new ideas, from wherever they come. The data, as explored in this book, proves overwhelmingly that immigrants are a vital source of entrepreneurial energy for a society, often starting businesses and opening up new streams of customers for their new country. From DuPont and Procter & Gamble to Google, Yahoo!, and eBay, the U.S. economy has long profited mightily from the entrepreneurial efforts of immigrants. An analysis done by the National Foundation for American Policy in 2011 found that, of the top fifty venture capital–backed companies in the country, twenty-four— just under half—were founded or cofounded by immigrants. The immigrant-founded companies in the survey employed an average of 153 people and were adding workers at the rate of twenty-seven employees a year. If we believe in free markets, we must extend that belief to labor markets as well and allow entrepreneurial people to seek opportunity across borders.

7. The Right to Be Different

Entrepreneurs come in all shapes, sizes, races, religions, and sexual orientations, with all kinds of abilities, disabilities, and personality types, from all walks of life and every corner of the globe.

As long as you can create something that fills a need and finds a market, you should have the right to pursue your entrepreneurial dream. Every person—no matter how unusual—has unique knowledge that could be turned into a successful business.

8. The Right to an Entrepreneurial Education

Entrepreneurship is a basic instinct of the human spirit, but it is not a weed that grows wild. It is a plant that only thrives when cared for and cultivated from a seedling. My restless, unmotivated students that fateful day at Boys and Girls High School in Bedford-Stuyvesant in 1981 had no idea of the power of entrepreneurship, no concept that they actually could start their own businesses. Nothing in their lives or schooling gave them the slightest intimation that such a thing was even possible. But when I held that watch up for their first business lesson, you could almost hear them growing. Owner-entrepreneurship education empowers young people to make well-informed decisions about their future, whether they choose to become entrepreneurs or not.

I describe myself as a libertarian in everything but this: Entrepreneurial education should be mandatory, for to deprive a child of the glimpse of the joy and value of starting a business is criminal. We must let disadvantaged youth worldwide in on the connection between ownership and wealth creation.

9. The Right to Overcome Obstacles

Entrepreneurs are the world's great problem solvers. One reason entrepreneurs are flourishing in the new digital age is that the flexibility the Internet demands is the same flexibility that a business owner has to demonstrate every working day. We don't have all the answers regarding what should be done in the next twenty, fifty, or one hundred years to promote entrepreneurship, because we don't know yet what the challenges will be. But we do know this: The Entrepreneurship Revolution will reward the agile and the imaginative, the visionaries and the problem solvers. Tomorrow's entrepreneurs deserve an economic system that frees them to replace obstacles with solutions and, in the process, create the wealth-building, job-creating businesses of the future.

10. The Right to Forge One's Own Path

The Entrepreneurship Revolution must be democratic, open to all. It may be the first revolution in history that won't have winners and losers—because it has the potential to make everyone better off without restricting anyone's freedom. This result, however, is not preordained: It's possible that Millennials—the generation coming of age in the twenty-first century—are less entrepreneurial in many ways than their parents. The rate of new business formation, as measured by the Kauffman Index of Entrepreneurial Activity, has barely budged in the last two decades. Self-employment rates among Americans ages twenty to twenty-four has declined, from 2.9 percent in 1977 to 1.7 percent in 2012, according to the Bureau of Labor Statistics. A new school of "innovation pessimists" even argues that the great job-creating tech revolution of the last three decades is slowing down and that there will be no more big breakthroughs.

I don't buy it. I think with the right mental mind-set, the right educational programs, the right government policies, and the right signals from the world's cultures, the global economy can put itself on a path for another unprecedented leap forward— this time to an age of unrivaled creativity and broadly shared wealth.

It's time to get to work.

Acknowledgments

———◆———

I WOULD LIKE TO THANK my writing partner, David Sands, for his in-depth research into the global state of entrepreneurship and his ability to organize and flesh out my ideas. I also thank Templeton Press publisher Susan Arellano; production manager Trish Vergilio; editorial and social media content coordinator Angelina Horst; and President and Chairman of the John Templeton Foundation Jack Templeton and his wife Pina for their friendship, advice and encouragement.

I am grateful to my long-term writing partner Debra DeSalvo for revising the manuscript and helping me add stories and history that further enriched the book, and to literary agent Jim Levine for finding the perfect publisher. In addition, I must thank Russ Carson for all our breakfast meetings discussing the role of the entrepreneur in society, Brianna Cregle for invaluable assistance, and friends who reviewed the manuscript and improved it, including Moushumi Kahn, Chris Locke, Michael Simmons and Paul Wisenthal. All the opinions and any errors that remain in this book are entirely my own.

In addition, I must thank all my wonderful students over the years for making me into a teacher. Watching you use entrepreneurship education to build wonderful lives for yourselves has been the greatest privilege of my life. I must thank all my colleagues at the Network for Teaching Entrepreneurship Inc. (NFTE) from the founding of the organization in 1987 to the present day, especially my brother Jack Mariotti and father John

Mariotti, for financing much of NFTE's early work and for their love and guidance. I also must acknowledge Michael Caslin, who brought organization to NFTE and discipline to the field of entrepreneurship education, and taught me the finer points of vision and leadership; and C.J. Meenan, who was instrumental in developing NFTE's teacher training and curriculum.

I commend NFTE's current leadership—Shawn Osborne, Kate Palmer Britton, Greg Cox, Dan Delaney, Thomas Gold, Lisa Miller, David White, Victor Salama, and Kim Smith—for the excellent job they are doing carrying forward NFTE's mission to provide entrepreneurship education programs worldwide that inspire young people from low-income communities to stay in school and create pathways for themselves from poverty to prosperity.

All NFTE's divisional directors have had a profound impact on the field of entrepreneurship education, and I am so proud of them and of our hundreds of hardworking and committed local board members in each city and country. Also crucial to NFTE's growth have been the efforts of Richard Fink of Koch Industries, Michie Slaughter of Ewing Marion Kauffman Foundation, Verne Harnish of Entrepreneurs' Organization, Tom Hartocollis of Microsoft Corporation, and Jean Thorne, Mike Hennessy, Julie and Marc Kantor, and John Hughes of The Coleman Foundation, Inc. NFTE could not have grown as it has without breakthrough insights into how to teach children to become business-literate from Clara Del Villar, Laurel Skurko, Bill Tkacs, Liza Vertinsky and Terry Mahoney, Ken Dillard, Cynthia Miree, Peter Janssen, Elizabeth Wright, Andrea Bonfils Leavitt, Christine Chambers, Janet McKinstry Cort, Leslie Koch, Jane Walsh, Sue Dubester, Carol Tully, Kathleen Kirkwood, and Dilia Wood.

I must also thank my early mentors and lifelong friends Ray Chambers and John C. Whitehead, and other visionary philanthropists who have funded NFTE, including Vicky and Max Kennedy, Charles and David Koch, Diana Davis Spencer of Shelby Cullom Davis Foundation, Karen Pritzker and The Seedlings Foundation, Scaife Family Foundation, Heinz Endowments, James H. Herbert, Jr. and First Republic Bancorp, William H. Donner Foundation, W. K. Kellogg Foundation, Koch Family Foundations, Richard King Mellon Foundation, The Clark Foundation, The New York Community Trust, The J. M. Kaplan Fund, Loida Nicolas-Lewis of Reginald F. Lewis Foundation, Argidius Foundation, Mary Myers Kauppila and our many wonderful anonymous donors.

This important work continues today under the guidance of NFTE's extraordinary board of directors: Maria Pinelli, Leonard A. Schlesinger, Peter J. Boni, Patrica Alper, Matthew J. Audette, Steven Birdsall, Ronald E. Garrow, Noah Hanft, Victor Oviedo, Jason Port, Amy Rosen, Anthon Salcito, Dia Simms, Diana Davis Spencer, David Spreng, Deryck van Rensburg, Peter B. Walker, Tucker York, and Sanford Krieger. I also want to acknowledge NFTE's terrific board of overseers: Stephanie Bell-Rose, Michelle Barmazel, Stephen Brenninkmeijer, Eddie Brown, Dr. Thomas Byers, Russ Carson, James I. Cash, Ray Chambers, Sean Combs, Mark Ein, Vince Gioe, Stedman Graham, Michael J. Hennessy, Landon Hilliard, Reid Hoffman, Daymond John, Moushumi Kahn, Elizabeth Koch, Loida Nicolas-Lewis, James Lyle, Dr. Richard K. Miller, Wes Moore, Alan Patricof, Jeffrey S. Raikes, Anthony Scaramucci, Jane Siebels, John P. Stack and Prof. Howard Stevenson.

Finally, I want to thank my mother, Nancy, a wonderful special-education teacher who showed me by example that one great teacher affects eternity.

Steve Mariotti

Index